'I HAVE SEEN THE LORD'

Witnesses of an Encounter with the Risen Christ

Edited by Rebecca Blakey, Cristóbal Valdés
& Martín Rosselot

Published by The Weave of Manquehue Prayer 2020

www.weaveofmanquehue.org

theweave@manquehue.org

Typeset and cover design by Antonia Weir

Cover illustration by Javiera Rojas Bontempi

In gratitude for the life and witness to Christ of Juanito Jiménez Borques (2007-2020)[1], whose Passover was celebrated on the sixth anniversary of his First Holy Communion during the preparations for this book.

'Length of days is not what makes age honourable, nor number of years the true measure of life; understanding, this is grey hairs, untarnished life, this is ripe old age. Having won God's favour, he has been loved'.
(Wisdom 4: 8-9)

---

1 Find more about Juanito in the testimony on page 26

CONTENTS

FOREWORD

Reading the testimonies in this UK edition of *I Have Seen The Lord* has filled me with joy and gratitude. It is moving to see the work of the Lord as it is experienced by people I know and by others I look forward to meeting in the future. It is God himself whose reflection I see in their words and experiences.

The testimonies have reminded me of my first visit to the United Kingdom and Ampleforth Abbey, a long time ago, because it was then that I started receiving echoes from the pupils as they did Lectio Divina. For many years, I have been nourished with the charism of the English Benedictine Congregation through echoes coming from men and women, young and old, monastic and lay. It has been a history of joy and unity in the Spirit with all those with whom I have shared along these years.

I take this opportunity to express my happiness to see The Weave of Manquehue Prayer come to life, because it is allowing many to come to know the Risen Christ through His Word and experience His salvation in this world. The Weave opens paths of evangelisation that we had not imagined, and it fills me with great hope because it is woven from human relationships, honest friendships, courageous mission, mutual support, and Christian formation. My hope is that through the perseverance and generosity of the people connected in the Weave, God will sow the seeds of a new Christianity that can give new life to the deepest roots of British identity and to the proclamation of the Gospel in today's world.

Let us praise the Lord for this book and be grateful to Him for those who undertook this initiative and for those who have contributed to it with their testimonies or with their work throughout the process of publication. The book will no doubt bring to many hearts in the United Kingdom and beyond, the living waters of the Word that come to us resounding through those who so generously share their testimonies with us.

> 'We cannot stop proclaiming what we have seen and heard.' (Acts 4:20)

> 'You are the light of the world. A city built on a hilltop cannot be hidden.' (Mt 5:14)

José Manuel Eguiguren
Responsable
Manquehue Apostolic Movement

INTRODUCTION

Dear reader,

We just can't tell you how glad we are that this book has come your way!

'I have seen the Lord' are the words with which Mary of Magdala tells the disciples that Jesus Christ is risen, that she has seen Him and that He has spoken to her (Jn 20:18). Christ is risen indeed! He did not die ever again after rising from the dead. The light and power of His resurrection have not been worn out by the centuries since the very first Easter morning. He is alive, and He comes forth today to meet people who can then proclaim with the same conviction and joy of Mary of Magdala: 'I have seen the Lord!'

This book is a compilation of testimonies from people who give witness to that. Each testimony is someone's attempt to share how they have seen the Lord, and how this has been important, even life changing, for them. They come in all sorts.

We have put them together in the hope that your life might be touched by Christ too. How we wish you could come to know Him! Whether it be for the very first time or once again; our own joy will then be complete.

If the stories in this book are true, then reality is not just what we see and the world is a very different place, infinitely better than we normally think. This is what this book is about. It is about meaning, purpose, joy, conviction, consolation, truth, way and life, found not in some ideas but in someone. We have had the gift of seeing many people, old and young, of all walks of life, come together to encounter the Lord, and to share, as friends, that awesome experience. We are inspired by seeing Jesus Christ alive and active in the lives of people, and eagerly wish to share these accounts of Good News with you.

Don't rush through the book, but read it slowly, maybe just one story each day. When reading, don't let yourself be put off by things of no substance, prejudices about people or misconceptions about religion. You may think you like or dislike those whose testimonies you read, but that is not important. Just bear in mind that their stories are true and that you can trust them because they are sharing disinterestedly with you.

This book is published by The Weave of Manquehue Prayer, a network of friends who seek to help one another to pray. The Weave is inspired by the Manquehue Apostolic Movement, a lay Benedictine community started in Chile and whose life breath is in Lectio Divina, the prayerful reading of Holy Scripture. For many years now, spiritual friendship has grown between Manquehue and the English Benedictine monasteries and schools. That is why you will find most of these testimonies unified by the Benedictine charism. The glossary at the end of the book may be of help if you happen to be unfamiliar with Benedictines or with Manquehue.

The circumstances in which this book came to exist are worth noting. Martín published his first book of testimonies when he was only fifteen and still a student at Colegio San Benito in Santiago de Chile. In March 2020 he came to the UK to take part in the life and mission of St Scholastica, the Manquehue community based at Downside. Two weeks later, all works of St Scholastica had to be revised and adapted to the new lockdown situation and the dormant project of an English version of the book was quickly brought back to life. At the same time, Rebecca found herself back in Scotland after a gap year in Chile that was cut short from five months to three weeks because of the pandemic and agreed enthusiastically to join the team of *I Have Seen The Lord*. We met online every week to pray and to work together. The pandemic, therefore, was not only a situation that was happening during the process, but also a mystery that pushed the project to occur and our friendship to grow.

Enjoy and God bless!

Rebecca, Martín & Cristóbal
The Weave of Manquehue Prayer

'WHAT YOU HEAR IN WHISPERS'
(Mt 10:27)

Theo Shack
St Willibrord Fellowship

'Do not be afraid. For everything that is now covered
will be uncovered, and everything now hidden will be
made clear. What I say to you in the dark, tell in the
daylight; what you hear in whispers, proclaim from
the rooftops.' (Mt 10:26-27)

It makes me feel vulnerable to write in the first person. I am
keen to universalise, partly because it takes the pressure off it
being just me, I feel less alone if I can imagine that the whole
of humanity must be on side.

The idea of writing a testimony is the opposite of that: it is
important and worth sharing precisely because it is personal,
it is just my encounter. Like an echo at Lectio.

I still have a way to go at recognising this. It is important
as a personal exclusive encounter because it speaks of my
unique relationship with God. Just as everybody has a unique
relationship – 'every hair on your head has been counted' (Mt

10:30). It is important also to share because together we are all one body in Christ.

In hearing His words in Matthew's Gospel above, I realise I am afraid; afraid to give a testimony, to hold the things that have been whispered to me and tell them from the rooftops. For in my way I feel that Christ has whispered things to me often, and once or twice, He has even proclaimed things straight from the rooftop into my ear, or heart. The temptation for me is to think only of these proclamations, the loudest moments, as being candidates for featuring in this book of testimonies. I am going to mention one, but the others I cannot share, and I think they are good to be covered for the moment, in the knowledge that they will be uncovered over time.

Another reason for this is that I do not want to take away from the significance of the whispers, because they are so many and so wonderful, and come with almost every encounter with the Word in Lectio. These, most of all, continue to be an incredible testament to the presence of God in the world for me. But now for the clarion call:

The first time I came to meet Manquehue was right at the start of January in 2019. My cousin, Rebecca, had told me about this retreat she was planning to attend and, right at the last minute, I decided to join her, sending a very hopeful email to Mary asking for my late admittance.

I came down on a Friday after work in January, arriving by train late at night to Bath, and was picked up by George. We arrived at Downside at around 9pm, and the rest of the members of the retreat had just finished praying Lectio. I arrived slightly rattled into this common room to be greeted warmly, which was in itself lovely, but significantly, their faces were glowing. Not visibly, as though fluorescent, but in some other way, in another facet or dimension. Sometimes holiness is visible in this way, or leaves its mark; after all, they'd just been in conversation with God, which is what Lectio is.

This might seem slight, or not that inspiring, but to me it was big. Very rarely indeed, does God so manifest Himself as to appear directly to the sense of sight, visible in this glowing.

When Mary Townsend came to visit our prayer group of St Willibrord in London, where we had recently started praying lectio, I told this story by way of introducing Mary and Lectio. At the time, she pointed towards when Moses comes down from Mt Sinai with the tablets and 'he was not aware that his face was radiant because he had spoken with the Lord' (Ex 34:29).

This was my first very powerful encounter with Christ in Lectio, and I hadn't even prayed Lectio yet. But it was clearly a strong endorsement. Since then, Christ speaks in the Gospels almost every time I pray Lectio with others. This certainly is a whispering, and the act of sharing an echo is only the small step on the way towards proclaiming Christ from the rooftops.

But the whispers are good. Sometimes, I think that Christ whispers so that I still have a chance to say it again afterwards, or act on it. If He spoke too loudly, there might be little left to do. And in hearing out for the whispering, I learn to listen more carefully.

My testimony really is this: I cannot exclaim enough how wonderful the practice of shared Lectio is. It is the way because Christ is the Way and Lectio is our way to encounter Christ.

'THROUGH HIM ALL THINGS CAME INTO BEING' (Jn 1:3)

Consuelo Verdugo Brito
Manquehue Apostolic Movement

I have seen the Lord so many times that I cannot count them. I have seen Him in the natural world, in the hills, seas and mountains. I have seen Him in the dawn of early morning, in the full moon shining joyfully for her Creator, at sunset, and also in the middle of the day, when the radiant sun sends out his brightness and heat; I have seen Him in the rain that refreshes the land and in the wind that whispers to me of God's Spirit. I have seen Him in the lakes, woods and deserts; in all things I have seen the Creator who reveals Himself and seems to call out to me in His work. I have seen the Lord who speaks to me strongly in His Word; He has made my heart burn within me so many times I cannot count them. He has accompanied, consoled, illuminated, corrected and motivated me; He has opened up horizons; He has filled me with force and energy, explained so many things and guided me; above all, He has loved me profoundly. I have seen Him in the liturgy and in so many Eucharists that have 'opened my eyes' to recognise Him in the breaking of the bread. I have seen Him in so many people: in my family, in my community, in the young, in pupils, in monks and nuns of the English Benedictine Congregation: in sharing the faith with them, in their echoes, in their affectionate actions and conversations, in their support, in their steadfastness. Above all, I have seen the Lord in spiritual friendship.

I have seen the Lord in my life, in how He has led and guided me to search for Him, each time, perhaps, with greater precision, to allow me to love and to be overwhelmed by His grace. I have seen Him creating a precious story with me that I would never, in my boldest imaginings, have foreseen for myself. I have seen Him in the gift of my community, in which I can live in deep friendship, which is a space that allows me to pray, do work that is meaningful, persevere and live in love. I have seen Him on the paths on which I have travelled, both in the sheltered valleys and in the dark ravines, because I have had times of dryness and difficulty; of loneliness, obscurity and many doubts; of feeling exceedingly poor and weak. But He has also led me along ways of profound love, into communities where we have lived out spiritual friendship, mission and evangelization with great apostolic zeal. He has given me times of formation and study, filling my life and vocation with meaning. He has given me tasks full of meaning and challenge. He has made sure that I have been sustained, supported, formed and guided by the community that has helped me to keep faithful to my vocation.

I have seen the Lord also in the many pilgrimages that He has granted me to make. I have visited many holy places that have enabled me to see the almighty and everlasting God acting in each one of them through His love. There I have met people who are very alive and real, close to us, who intercede for me, inspiring me to follow their steps: Benedict and Scholastica; Aelred; Cuthbert; Columba; Aidan; Hilda; Jerome; Gregory the Great; Peter; Paul; Teresita of the Andes and Thérèse of Lisieux; Ignatius of Antioch; Francisca Romana; James the Great; John Paul II. They are all my close friends today, through whom the Lord has granted me to renew my faith and vocation at their tombs or holy places. He has enabled me to feel them alive, fully alive; these have been moments of touching eternity.

My name is Consuelo Verdugo (Chelo). I am a coenobitic oblate of the Manquehue Movement. I have made a life-long promise that helps me in my intention of seeking to live my baptism profoundly in the spirit of St Benedict and in fidelity to the Church. I am a former pupil of one of the Manquehue schools. It has been my good fortune to hear the proclamation of the Word of God and to encounter Jesus Christ, fully alive in that Word. Lectio and friendship led me to my vocation.

Shortly before deciding on my vocation, I was engaged in Lectio on the Gospel of the day. I was alone in a remote office on the third floor of San Benito School. It was the Feast of the Transfiguration of the Lord. I was not able to concentrate, and, in the end, my eyes strayed to the other page of the Bible. The words I found there pierced my heart like a sword:

'If anyone wants to be a follower of mine, let him renounce himself and take up his cross and follow me. Anyone who wants to save his life will lose it; but anyone who loses his life for my sake will find it. What, then, will anyone gain by winning the whole world and forfeiting his life? Or what can anyone offer in exchange for his life?' (Mt 16:4-26)

Those words transfigured my heart. It was clear to me that I wanted to 'lose' my life in the eyes of the world because the Lord – and I had already had a foretaste of this – wanted to give me life in abundance; He wanted to fill my heart with His love, with His peace and His strength. I would not lose anything; on the contrary, I would gain everything by taking that step of trust and by abandoning myself into His hands. I felt afraid. It was not easy for me to work out what I wanted to do about my family and friends. I did not have any persuasive arguments, and to say, 'It is what God is saying to me' did not sound convincing. This fear was starting to grow inside me; it began to persuade me that perhaps it would not be necessary to take a public step and that what I was doing by way of a series of readings that had come my way was without a rational foundation. It was then that I decided to take a final random reading. I would do what that reading said to me. I called upon the Holy Spirit, opened my Bible, and read:

'In the beginning was the Word: the Word was with God and the Word was God. He was with God in the beginning. Through him all things came into being, not one thing came into being except through him. What

has come into being in him was life, life that was the
light of men; and light shines in darkness, and darkness
could not overpower it.' (Jn 1:1-5)

There was no need to read on. If God had created ALL
THINGS through His Word, He had also created my vocation
in and through His Word. I was flooded with peace when I
saw that God was calling me to be part of this Manquehue
Community. Yet I also experienced nervousness that only
the certainty that God was guiding me and urging me to go
forward could overcome. From that time onwards, I have
continued to see the Lord on numberless occasions.

He also made me see Him in the gift of being part of the
Saint Scholastica Community at Downside for three years.
God used Downside to transfigure my heart anew. I shall never
forget arriving in Stratton-on-the-Fosse in the cold and gloom
of a late January. The place scared me. I encountered vast and
imposing buildings, polite pupils and a monastic community
with a long tradition. The shock was all the greater because
I had just come from living in a simple rural community in
Chilean Patagonia. Gradually, through the love of so many
people and in prayer, my heart was 'transfigured', changing my
outlook and showing me that those enormous buildings were
in reality temples full of the Holy Spirit, full of his praise and
prayer. In those intimidating pupils I discovered young people
with a thirst for God, whose eyes shone each time they shared
an echo or sang with power those hymns at Sunday Mass. In
the monastic community, I discovered dear friends who, with
their witness of fidelity, perseverance and rootedness, showed

me that not only was it possible to live their vocation, but that it was a gift and Life.

I would need books to tell of the gifts that have stayed with me since the day I arrived in England. The gifts of precious friendship, the support and mission shared with so many young people who have had a Gap Year in Chile as well as with other alumni of the EBC schools. The gifts that were the visitors to the community, the retreats that we organised, their testimonies of devotion and generosity. These friends set up groups for Lectio in universities; their love and fidelity to the Word filled me with God's Spirit, with His Life and love. To top it all, I witnessed the birth of The Weave of Manquehue Prayer. This has been one more gift that I treasure in my heart. Its life and intensity, its seriousness and power, its rootedness and perseverance, fill me with awe and I can only say, 'We have seen strange things today' (Lk 5:26).

The Lord continues to manifest Himself with power today. I discover each day that God is keeping back for me, just as at Cana, the good wine of life and of His call (Jn 2:10). I have not yet seen the half of what God has given me (2 Ch 9:6).

MORE THAN 'JUST PRAYING'

Alex

Downside School

> 'My friend, move up higher. Then everyone with you
> at the table will see you honoured. For everyone who
> raises himself up will be humbled, and the one who
> humbles himself will be raised up.' (Lk 14:10-11)

Upon writing this testimony I wondered how I might start.
I used a classic trick the St Scholastica community here at
Downside have taught me. I flicked to a random page of the
New Testament and read where my finger landed. This is a
snippet of the passage I stumbled upon. In it, Jesus teaches us
to put others in front of and above ourselves. This is one of
my favourites of the Benedictine values that we practise in our
community: 'Humility'.

This community I speak of is my Lectio community, one
where I have learned to 'see the Lord', in Scripture and in
the way God speaks to me through others. Doing this has
changed my life, and this is the story of how it happened.

Throughout my whole life, I have always been exposed to the idea of God and religion. I was baptised Catholic as a baby, followed by receiving the sacraments of Reconciliation and First Holy Communion in my childhood. By the age of eight, I had received nearly half of the sacraments. One might have said, 'What a good Catholic boy he is, he goes to mass every Sunday to receive the Eucharist and Word, and reconciles his sins as often as he can'. You would have thought that by the age of eleven I would have had at least one encounter with God. In a way, I did; I prayed every night and followed what my family did in all religious aspects (apart from marriage, I was a bit too young for that!) and those encounters were real and good. But I never questioned any of it for myself. I was a sheep following the flock without any realisation of what my faith really meant.

When I entered Downside School as a first former, I knew that there would be mass every Sunday, Hymn Practice and other prayer services but I had never heard of Lectio Divina. When I was first introduced to Lectio by a Prefect, my first thought was, 'Great. More praying.' I already prayed in my own time anyway, why would I need to do more praying? However, I went along with it as it was my first week and there was the attraction of free food.

Aside from getting free food, however, I discovered that Lectio Divina was not 'just praying' — it was so much more than that. It was different from any type of prayer I had done before. We read a passage from the Gospel, and then went round in a circle, taking turns to 'share an echo' — this means to answer the question: 'what strikes you personally in this passage?' For the first time in my life, I didn't know what to say. No one had ever asked me to share what I thought about God before. I felt challenged and did not say anything at first. I was scared to share something personal with people I had only known for two or three days. What if they disagree with me? What if they judge me? What if I do not make any sense? These were all questions spinning through my head. When the Lectio leader asked if anyone wanted to say anything more, I felt the need to speak out and say something. I gave my echo and shared my private thoughts with people I hardly knew. But it felt good. I felt as if I was professing my faith for the first time and sharing it.

For most of my school journey, I did Lectio every week. Eating, talking and praying with friends helped me to grow more than ever before in my faith. However, it was not all easy. I still had my doubts about God. Through studying philosophy, where we questioned the very concept of God, my once-simple faith was challenged and completely changed from how I had originally understood it. As an early teenager, I had been naïve and thought I knew everything there was to know about God, but by the age of fourteen, I did not feel like I knew Him anymore. How could He create a world with so much suffering? I still went to mass but was always distracted; I felt it was pointless and not worth my time. However, despite feeling torn away from my faith, I still had a deep-seated belief in God and wanted to reconnect with Him. I realised that in my third form year I had not been in a Lectio group and wondered whether that was why I had lost my way. Perhaps, I thought, my strong faith in God had been sourced from doing Lectio in community. In the summer term of third form, a new Lectio group was formed and I joined straight away to test my theory. I realised the moment our first meeting ended that my guess had been correct. I had deeply missed praying and sharing my echoes with community members. From then on I was a committed member.

In fifth form, I was invited to become a Lectio leader. My friend and I led a group of second formers and it was a new challenge to encourage younger pupils to participate in Lectio, but I had always hoped I might become a Lectio leader, and felt prepared for the challenge, and ready to spread the word. As a Lectio leader, I was also invited to join a group called St John's, the group consisting of all other Lectio leaders in the school. We met every Thursday night and I liked having more than one chance to do Lectio in a week. I was always excited to go to the meetings and continue to pray with friends. I have been a Lectio leader for two years now and plan to continue in my upcoming final year. Through my time at Downside, I believe I have truly encountered God, especially through Lectio, which is essentially a fun time to eat, talk and pray with friends. But it is a deeper and more significant event than that and through it I have found God.

There might be someone reading this who feels they have never had an encounter with God or has, like me, been raised religiously but feels they have not truly been inspired yet. If that's you, I strongly encourage you to participate in a Lectio group. It is a great opportunity to find God, and, if you have no Lectio groups around you, I encourage you to form your own and invite people to do Lectio with you.

'LOOK TO THE LORD AND BE RADIANT' (Ps 34: 5)

Mary Townsend (Hirst)
The Weave of Manquehue Prayer

My name is Mary and I am twenty-five years old and I live in York. A couple of weeks ago on the feast of St Benedict, I got married to my best friend whom I met at Ampleforth, a Benedictine school in Yorkshire. It was also at Ampleforth that I met Manquehue; a friendship which has lasted many years now and has included a lot of time living in different Manquehue communities. Before getting married I lived and worked at Downside school for two years as part of the Community of St Scholastica. The community had been a big part of my life when I was at university; I am very struck by how the Lord later called me to spend time there accompanying others as I too had been accompanied. When I finished school I spent six months living in the Manquehue women's house, San Jeronimo, just outside of Santiago. After studying Theology at Oxford University I returned to Chile again, this time to spend time in Patagonia with the community there. While back in the UK I have also been involved with The Weave of Manquehue Prayer and very much hope to continue to be!

Looking back now in writing this, it is with a very grateful heart because the Lord has shown His love to me many, many times and through countless friendships and people. Being taught to pray is, I think, the most important thing that has led me to be able to say with Mary of Magdala 'I have seen the Lord'. It is only with prayer that I could ever say these words and it is difficult to put into words or express what this means for me. I can say that it was my parents, particularly my mother, who taught me to pray. Specifically my mother taught me to talk, to 'chat', to Jesus as my friend. Later, I was taught how to pray Lectio Divina and this transformed my prayer life into a place where I learn to deepen my listening to God – not only chatting to Him! It also teaches me to recognise Him in places I might not expect and I continually discover what He is like. It is a real miracle to me that He would want to reveal Himself to me and not only that but to discover that He is interested even in the minutiae of my life, details I would think too boring or trivial for anyone else. He's heard my deepest desires and, even with knowing all of my thoughts and all my actions, He loves me.

A time where 'I have seen the Lord', was after morning prayer with my community in Chile, praying alone in the chapel. I was praying in a very simple way for my family who were on the other side of the world from me at that time – the unity that comes with prayer became a very real experience for me as I spent those months far away from many whom I love. As I was praying, I was suddenly overcome by a great desire to laugh, to giggle. This was followed by an overwhelming awareness of the fact that I was not only by myself, but in the chapel, a place where I had always been taught that I should be reverent and respectful. While I tried my utmost to be quiet, I couldn't stop laughing and I was sent into further, completely irrepressible, giggles at the realisation that it was the Lord who was making me laugh – in church! I had the image of a father (my father-in-law in fact) with a child on his knee (my young brother-in-law) bouncing him and making him giggle. The father was giggling and the child was catching his laughter. This was exactly what was happening to me. The Lord was laughing and I was catching that laughter and we were both weeping with that laughter together. The Lord was cheering me up! I had not realised that I needed this, though clearly I did, and I think He has set me laughing ever since.

This moment was a very deep and joyful experience of God's love for me. It brought me very close to my husband who, though very far away from me at the time, had told me a year previously 'God has the best sense of humour'. He was very clearly right! I also could not keep His gift of joy to myself. It allowed me to exclaim as with Sarah in the Bible, 'God has given me cause to laugh! All who hear about this will laugh with me!' (Gn 21: 6). I had always been somewhat afraid of sharing my friendship with God, not wanting to alienate people or for them to think I was strange. But here the Lord gave me something that, somehow, I was able to share and it was a real multiplication of joy in the way that people would laugh with me when I told them. They recognised the Lord too and found that He was laughing with and rejoicing in them also. I had many laughing conversations in the days that followed!

Since then I have even more of a desire to share His love, His joy, His laughter with others and I also realise how much and how often the Lord goes about cheering me up. I can be very downhearted sometimes! Not in the Lord. St Paul says, 'Always be joyful, then, in the Lord, I repeat, be joyful' (Ph 4:4). For me this joy is something that comes from Christ, not simply an emotion or feeling but it comes with a call for me to decide to be joyful. To choose Him. To love Him. A calling I have to answer and a choice I have to make every day – more than once! What a vocation!

For anyone reading this I can only say Pray! And smile! 'Look to the Lord and be radiant' (Ps 34:5). The Lord has so much of Himself that He wants to share with you and for you, in turn, in your own entirely unique way, to share with others. Rejoice in Him because 'God is love, and whoever remains in love remains in God and God in him.' (1 Jn 4:16b).

'YOU ARE THE LIGHT OF THE WORLD' (Mt 5:14)

Pedro Vega Rivadeneira
Manquehue Apostolic Movement

My name is Pedro Vega and I am twenty-two years old. I graduated in 2015 from San Anselmo, one of the schools of the Manquehue Apostolic Movement, and now I'm studying Electrical Engineering at university in Santiago, Chile's capital. I think that I have to start with when I was born, because I have a chronic heart disease called Hypoplasia in the left ventricle. I can't explain what it actually is, but because of that, my parents had to travel to the United States for my birth. I needed a rare surgery which was safer to do in the USA than in Chile. In the end, I had three surgeries, but the important part is that before the first one I was baptised, just in case something went wrong, and after the third one, I was baptised again with all my family in Chile. I don't know if you actually can get baptised twice, because, I don't know, maybe the second one annuls the first one. But I think for me this is really important, because who knows what would have happened if I had not been baptised the first time? So, for me, this was my first real encounter with God, His first manifestation of himself to me. Although I, of course, don't remember it, I feel like He saved me and gave me the gift of life in a special way.

When I was a freshman I went to a Manquehue retreat, and it was there that I learned how to do Lectio and where I discovered my favourite verse of the bible: it is Matthew 5:14, which says: 'You are the light of the world. A city built on a hill-top cannot be hidden', and it has been really important for me, especially the first part, because since that day I always felt called to something different. It is impressive how this verse, in a way, has guided me for many years, because I've always had it in mind. For me it has been really important to have a little word of God that always illuminates me, and it cheers me up every time I read it.

It was also during that same year that I started my Lectio group with my friends. This has been really important in my life for many reasons. First, we met every week for about six years. So these guys became my best friends, the people who I came to trust even more than my own family; I can now talk with them about anything, because I've known them for so long. But it's also because, for me, it is not just any friendship: it is what we in Manquehue call a spiritual friendship, which goes further than just having fun or going out to parties together. It has been really important to have a community of friends like that, because I can find the support that I can't find anywhere else, and even though we don´t do Lectio together any more, all the times we have done it has changed our relationship forever.

Then in the summer of 2014 (December to February in Chile), when I was going from Sophomore to Junior Year, I experienced the 'trabajos y misiones' of San Anselmo, which translates roughly to 'work and missions'. This is an activity for people from Freshman to Senior years and alumni of the school, and that summer I went for the first time. It's a bit like a retreat, which happens every winter and summer, lasting either ten days or seven. We go to poor areas in Chile to build emergency houses for people that don't have anywhere to live, and we also go house by house, getting to know the people there and praying with them, sharing a passage and having a chat. We experience community life based on the rule of Saint Benedict, praying the Liturgy of the Hours, doing lectio every day and other kinds of stuff based on the charism of Manquehue. I'm telling you this just for you to try to understand this experience, but also because for me, this experience changed my life.

You can't imagine the conditions in which some people actually live and, coming from a good neighbourhood, I found the contrast between my own life and the poverty I saw during this time really shocking. However, there is something that I found more shocking than that, and it was that these people, in most cases, were, believe it or not, some of the happiest people I had ever met. Watching them living their faith happily, in spite of all the difficulties in their lives, made me realise that everything that the 'world' wants me to do –

study the best career to have the best job and earn as much money as I can – are not in themselves going to lead to true happiness. Luke says in his gospel:

> 'Therefore I tell you, do not worry about your life, what you will eat; or about your body, what you will wear. For life is more than food, and the body more than clothes.' (Lk 12:23)

To see how happy these people were really changed me. It made me want to seek true happiness and, from what I have learnt, that comes from sharing my faith and giving my life to others.

So, the experience I had in 'trabajos y misiones' had a huge impact on me and made me who I am now, as I learned the happiness of giving service and thinking about others more than myself, as Matthew says in his gospel;

> 'In the same way your light must shine in the sight of men, so that, seeing your good works, they may give the praise to your Father in heaven.' (Mt 5:16)

Also, I learned how important it is to always come back to God, His presence and His commandments. As a senior, I decided to join a community called 'Escuela de Servicio San Anselmo' (San Anselmo Service School), which meets every week, organises 'trabajos y misiones' and tries to live in a spirit of mission and service during the year. I've been in this community for almost five years and I can truly say that it has made 'service' my vocation. I have found the happiness that

comes when I share a common mission and practise my faith
with others at the same time.

In 2017 I did a mission to Ampleforth School with the
Manquehue, for four months. There is a lot I could say about
my time there but I will just say that it helped me to realise
something really important that comes from the gospel of
John; it says:

> 'You did not choose me, no, I chose you; and I
> commissioned you to go and to bear fruit, fruit that
> will last' (Jn 15:16).

I don't know why I decided to go to Ampleforth but I can
say that it was God who made the decision for me. In going
there, I realised that it is the Holy Spirit who acts through me,
in the way John also describes in his gospel:

> 'The wind blows wherever it pleases; you cannot tell
> where it comes from or where it is going. That is how
> it is with all who are born of the Spirit.' (Jn 3:8)

After realising this, the only thing I think I can do is just give
my life to God and just let Him do whatever He wants from
today and forever.

Finally, this past summer I went to Portsmouth in the
USA, again as a missionary for Manquehue and again trying
to follow this Holy Spirit that has the biggest but unknown
plans for me. I have to say that it was the best experience
I have ever had, and, just as with Ampleforth, there is a lot
I could tell you, but I'll just say that I really lived a phrase of
Saint Benedict. 'Today is Easter', he says in the second book of

dialogues, giving an invitation to live every day with the same joy, same spirit in which we celebrate Easter. This exhortation was our community guide for the whole experience, as we only concerned ourselves with the present – as a Chilean comedian used to say, the present is called present because it is a gift!

Saint Paul wrote to the Romans:

> 'But, now you are set free from sin and bound to the service of God, your gain will be sanctification and the end will be eternal life.' (Rm 6:22)

For me, this verse, which speaks about the service of God, the gain of which is sanctification, really makes a lot of sense in the face of all my own life encounters with Him. I feel called to live as a saint, to do everything as a saint, especially knowing that the end will be eternal life; so basically, it'll be no end.

'CHRIST VISITING CHRIST'

Dom Leo Maidlow Davis OSB
Downside Abbey

'My dear friends, we are already God's children, but what we shall be in the future has not yet been revealed'. (1 Jn 3:2)

In March 2014, I flew out to Chile at the end of an eleven-year period as Headmaster of Downside School. I had been a pupil in the school myself, before entering the monastic community in 1975. I first encountered the Manquehue Apostolic Movement through Abbot Richard Yeo, who told me of the impressive way in which they were able to share the Good News of Eternal Life in their schools and other projects. He gave me a set of their documents, but I could not then read Spanish and I was preoccupied with the tasks that beset a new Headmaster. Then, in 2005, Cristián Destuet and some young people from Chile came to spend two months in the school, introducing the ideas of Lectio Divina and Tutoría to the pupils. Although there were some who said that what worked in Chile could never work in England, I sensed, though

I did not understand much about it, that what these young people were bringing was good and helpful.

Over the next decade my knowledge of and respect for the work of the Manquehue Apostolic Movement deepened and developed. I had the privilege of being able to make several trips to Chile to find out more about the Movement and, still more importantly, to grow in friendship with its Responsable, José Manuel Eguiguren, and many other Oblates and friends of the Movement. Back at Downside, the sharing of Lectio Divina, the building of spiritual friendship groups and even fraternal correction became established parts of life and ones in which I engaged as much as I could. So, when I retired as Headmaster and was told by Abbot Aidan Bellenger that I could have a time away from Downside, I had no difficulty in making up my mind to ask for a longer stay in Chile. I hoped I could be of some help there as a monk and a priest, but I had little clear idea of a plan and was besides glad to be free of plans for a while. More deeply, I think, I had a sense that the link between Downside Monastery and School and the Manquehue Apostolic Movement was a providential work of the Holy Spirit with which I should try to cooperate.

There is one encounter in particular during that stay I would like to tell you about. It was suggested that I might join a small group of ladies attached to San Lorenzo School, whose Lectio community is dedicated to Santa María en Sábado; they meet on Wednesday mornings for Lectio Divina and then go out to visit the sick or those who would appreciate a visit who live around the school. Recoleta is a densely populated area where families live in houses that they appear to have built for themselves and where property has to be protected and defended. Everyone has a large dog or two and each house is enclosed behind a kind of cage of iron railings and screens. Yet this defensive impression is softened by the trees that grow by the side of the roads and the view of the snow-capped mountains that surround Santiago and which you can almost always see when you lift up your eyes. Many of the inhabitants have moved in from the country, and their houses are made delightful by the presence of their animals and plants; one lady was sharing her front room with her chickens. But what struck me most as we walked through the streets was the welcome and friendship extended to our little group. Kristin, Juanita, Teresita and Rosita were obviously well known for their visiting of the sick and elderly, while I was respected as a priest carrying the Blessed Sacrament and the Holy Oils. It was common for passers-by to greet us in the street and ask for a blessing.

One April day, Silvia Torrejón took me to visit a little boy called Juanito, who was suffering from leukaemia. His home, which he shares with his mother Claudia, his brother Carlitos, and his grandfather, stands opposite the main gates of San Lorenzo School. We found Juanito, who was then six years old, cheerful, but frail. His treatment had caused the loss of his hair. My spoken Spanish hardly existed and I understood little of what people said, but we could communicate through the prayers, which I was able to read more or less intelligibly. I laid hands on Juanito and prayed for his cure. In return, he showed me an old crucifix, given him, I believe, by his grandfather. Claudia told me that he always took it with him when he went to hospital for his treatment sessions. On a later visit, I administered the Sacrament of the Sick to Juanito and anointed him. He listened intently to the Gospel and then, when one of the ladies from the Lectio group asked if he had any prayer intentions, he replied, 'I would like us to pray for the other children who have cancer and who are suffering more than me.' That reply, in which he asked not for his own healing, though he must have longed for it, but for others, made a deep impression on me, and I think we who were present felt that Christ had come very close to us.

Afterwards I fell to thinking that if I could administer the Sacrament of the Sick to Juanito, then I ought also to be able to bring Christ to him in the Blessed Sacrament. I talked this idea over with the members of the Lectio group, and they suggested that I should call on Patricia Jara, the Head Mistress of San Lorenzo, for her advice. When we met, Patricia pointed out that Juanito would not normally make his First Holy Communion for another two years, and he might be frightened that we were expecting him to die. I reflected on this for a time and then said something like, 'We're all going to die. The sacraments give us eternal life; they are not intended to kill us.' Patricia agreed, adding that Juanito had extra time because of his sickness and absence from school for treatment and that it would be quite possible to prepare him carefully for his First Holy Communion. However, we would need to ask his mother what she thought. A few days passed, during which

I felt impatience; I was therefore delighted when I heard that Claudia and Juanito were happy to make the preparations.

Because I could not speak Spanish, others instructed Juanito, and a special Mass was arranged in the chapel in San Lorenzo School. We gathered there on the morning of Friday June 20th, a cold and foggy midwinter's day. I was due to depart from Chile on June 22nd, and so this was a culminating moment of my stay. Because of my poor Spanish, Fr Christian Reyes came to hear Juanito's first confession and to preside at the Mass. Juanito looked apprehensive. He was dressed in an alb with its hood up and was wearing a face-mask as he was so susceptible to infection. The congregation, who had gathered especially for the occasion, was large. Juanito's family had come, taking time off work, as well as all the children from Juanito's class and the class of his brother Carlitos. Kristin and the ladies from her lectio group were there as well as a number of Oblates and friends who had come with flowers and to help with the music and everything that would make Juanito's First Communion a joyful day. Fr Cristián quickly dissipated any nervousness; he asked the children questions, to which they offered eager replies. In his sermon, he said that Juanito and his family were sharing in the suffering and tears of Christ, and in His resurrection.

At the end of the Mass, there was applause. Fr Cristián handed Juanito the microphone, inviting him to say a word of thanks to everyone who had come. A kind person stood by me to translate. Juanito looked very happy but tired; standing during the Mass must have been demanding for him. Then he said, 'Thank you for coming. I have too much love to be able to tell you.'

That day and those words are something I shall never forget. Although I had been a monk and a priest for nearly forty years, Juanito had shown me the love of Christ in a new and deeper way than I had ever experienced it before. I recognised that, through Juanito, Christ was speaking to us all.

Afterwards Kristin had a conversation with me about the Lectio group and its visits in the neighbourhood that I would also like to share with you. She told me that the group had been visiting the sick and distressed for six years. Each visit must begin with Lectio divina because the visits are not social-work projects. Rather, Christ is visiting Christ. Some visits take the group members into distressing situations where they can see no way of helping. Kristin said it is important at such times not to keep what you have seen and heard locked inside yourself; it is too much to cope with and can even make you ill. So afterwards, back in the school chapel for Midday Prayer or Mass, the members of the group hand everything back to Christ, who knows what to do. As I listened to Kristin, I realised that I had seen the truth of her words in action on that unforgettable day.

N.B. Juanito Jiménez Borques died while this book was being prepared on 19th June 2020. His funeral Mass was celebrated the next day in the chapel at San Lorenzo School. It was the sixth anniversary of his First Holy Communion. Juanito has now entered completely into the 'too much love' of Our Lord Jesus Christ.

'I ASKED TO BE GOD'S VESSEL'

Joanna Doliwa
The Weave of Manquehue Prayer

I find myself very blessed to have believed in God ever since I can remember. I was brought up as a Catholic, but my family was not very conservative about the faith. We would go to a Sunday Mass every once in a while, but not every single week and the times when we prayed together at home were mainly limited to Easter and Christmas. I would say though, that my childhood faith was more than just repeating Hail Marys or singing songs about Noah's ark in my general religion classes. When the time came for my First Holy Communion, I tried to prepare my heart to open to Jesus in a new way as well as I could at the age of eight.

I carried on with being faithful, praying sometimes more, sometimes less, and having moments when I thought I was really close to God as well as ones when I felt not strong enough to follow Him. At the age of around thirteen or fourteen I found myself very unsure of who I actually was; I wondered about other people or how I would define myself. Not knowing where I belonged or what I should be like, I tried to fit in with the people around me, and although they weren't bad people I felt like I wasn't happy being who I became around them. At the back of my mind I still had Jesus, who according to the Bible and my religion teachers was supposed to know me better than I did myself. Every time I made the effort to sustain a meaningful relationship with Him though, I eventually failed. I think that might have been because I did not have a person that would direct me back to Him when I wasn't strong enough to do it myself. As it turned out later, I really needed to be a part of a community.

A major breakthrough in my faith came during the preparation for my Confirmation. I went on a weekend retreat to a local retreat centre in the countryside, together with some of my classmates and people from the parish in which I was to be confirmed. At that point I was really fed up with who I was – I struggled to be the same person around different people; I felt like some of my relationships were meaningless and that I didn't know how to change myself to feel happier and be more at peace. And then it happened – the Saturday evening prayer. After the event, my religion teacher, who played the guitar that night, would say to me: 'You know, you were supposed to accompany the singing with your violin playing, but after maybe one song, you disappeared'. I hadn't actually left, but I did indeed abandon the violin-playing quite quickly. I remember that at one point I just looked at the Blessed Sacrament placed in the middle of the chapel and felt that God wanted to change something in my life through that prayer. All He desired me to do was just agree to what He had prepared for me that evening. And I did.

For the first time I honestly told Him how unhappy and lost I was, and that I had tried to change but couldn't. And then I started to wish I was like Jesus – so humble, helpful, kind, and peaceful. Shortly after, a realisation came – if I can't change to be like that on my own, surely the Holy Spirit can help me. During that prayer I asked to be God's vessel. I told Him I didn't want anything I did to come from me; I wanted to be empty for Him to fill me with His Spirit. That I wanted Him to be present within me every single day of my life, to direct it in His way, not mine, and make me be similar to Christ. That evening truly changed me as a person and at the end of it words from the Gospel came to my mind: 'nobody puts new wine in old wineskins […] nobody who has been drinking old wine wants new. "The old is good", he says'. (Lk 5:37;39) For me that meant not returning to life as it was before the prayer, to 'fitting-in with people surrounding me' and 'looking down on others because that's a social norm in middle school', which could at times be very easy. The 'new wineskin' was choosing God every day, letting Him speak through me and allowing Him to use my hands for His actions. This is not saying I haven't sinned again – I did many, many times, but since then I have been better able to recognise my sins for what they are and seek forgiveness.

'Not drinking old wine' had been made easier by joining a community of young people at the same parish where my

Confirmation took place. Going there every Friday motivated me to stay close to God and deepen my faith. Moreover, I met people who I could share my thoughts and beliefs with, and I became a leader for retreats for younger school years. I will also forever remember the joyful singing together and the Christmas Eve celebrations I experienced while being a part of that community. Later on, I came to Downside for 6th form and shared my encounter with Christ by being a Lectio and Tutoria leader.

Even though my friendship with God has been very fruitful, I sometimes still find it difficult to be close to Him always, but every time I do, I know I have to trust the Holy Spirit to do the things not as I desire them to be but how He planned. One of my greatest struggles is thinking that I am not good enough to be His instrument, that when others meet me and realise that I am a Catholic they will get a very deformed image of what Jesus is really like. This is something I am battling through and this is the battle I often lose.

Yet every time I come back to start again, instead of words of punishment or anger I hear 'I love you'. And it is that love that made Jesus die for me on the cross that encourages me to keep trying to become a better and more selfless person. Some people say that religion and faith greatly limit people as they have to follow certain rules. My experience is very different – through faith I gain freedom to distinguish the good from the bad and decide which one I choose. Through faith and the gifts of the Holy Spirit I gain the courage to not follow the crowd if I disagree with it, and am able to go out of my comfort zone to show compassion. It is thanks to religious practices such as going to Mass and reciting the rosary that I understand the meaning of life more deeply and can notice beauty and love in suffering. And it is thanks to doing Lectio that I learn to see people through Jesus' eyes, which are full of understanding and love.

THE GRACES OF GOD

George Rawlins
The Weave of Manquehue Prayer

I felt lost, confused, and full of love for someone far away, a 'missed-place' love. I had been in Patagonia for a month and a half. Something in my heart was out of focus and I was beginning to get frustrated with God in my complete lack of understanding: 'My God, My God, why Lord have you forsaken me?' (Ps 22:1a) for 'into your hands I commend my spirit' (Lk 23:46). These words fell from my lips with even more passion, honesty and belief than ever before.

Over three years before that moment, at the age of seventeen, I went to the Christmas Vigil in a cold coastal town. We entered the church just as the priest began Mass. My half-distracted-self had been committed to going – I had been the one to ask my parents to take me and we had left the rest of the family at home. It was during the homily that something stirred in my heart and for a moment I asked myself the question: 'Do you, George, believe in God: "yes" or "no"?' The stirring in my heart didn't require a complicated answer of 'yes, but…' or 'no because'. In that moment, I just had to answer the question with a 'yes' or a 'no'. For what I would now call a grace of the Holy Spirit, I said 'yes' with the conviction that nothing else, no arguments that I could muster, would be enough to change my answer.

A few weeks later I returned to Downside, to a familiar rhythm, but something significant had changed in my heart – understanding and desire had refocused itself within me. This is when I received a second grace from God on my path of conversion: Lectio Divina. I was shown a way to have conversation with God, to hear His word in my life today, to hear Him in my new-found heart of love. What surprised me at the time was that I didn't do it alone but surrounded by my friends and within the Monastic heartbeat of Downside. Through them I could listen to the word of love from God in their lives (whether they acknowledged it or not). By this second grace, God became more familiar, a friendly and engaging presence that I found easy to encounter in the world in which I lived.

For me, school was an environment where the presence of God wasn't only apparent to me in the relationship I had with the monks or in the constant opportunities to pray, but also in the life of the wider school community (friends, housemates, staff) with whom I spent my entire day. My life after school, when I moved to a city to enter the world of work at the age of eighteen, and was released into the unknown, was a real contrast.

In these early years of my career and life in a new city, I was caught by God once again in what to me felt like a complete chance encounter but must have been part of His plan for me to rediscover His friendship: I was invited to join a Lectio Group. More than just an opportunity to read God's Word together, with this group of people I was in the presence of friends (beers, touch rugby, the odd play-fight), I glimpsed community life and, most importantly at that time, received the invitation to pray.

This invitation led me to begin to recite the 'Night Prayer' of the Church regularly, no matter where I was. Anyone who has worked away in another city will be familiar with the loneliness that this 'hotel life' offers. For me, the void was a blessing. I felt it was an opportunity to fill it with constant and continuous prayer to God – not that I did this enough but at least I had the comfort of being able to turn to God and pray Night Prayer whenever I felt loneliness. In this new-found relationship with God, the following words were an expression of His comfort:

> 'So do not worry about tomorrow: tomorrow will take care of itself. Each day has enough trouble of its own.' (Mt 6:34)

The conversations, opportunity to pray, and the love of God that I felt at the time were all leading me to a clear conclusion – that I must allow time in my life for God to talk to me more clearly. I had experienced moments of joy, encounter, and felt the love of God like an embrace over numerous retreats, visits, testimonies, intense prayer and friendships. I felt called to make a greater act of commitment to him. So I asked for time off work, planned a sabbatical and left England for Manquehue's Retreat house in Patagonia.

At the point where everything was planned, organised, and committed to God, I received a third grace in my life: love. I met my now-girlfriend just less than six months before I was due to leave for Patagonia. In meeting her, it felt like my steady path of conversion had been turned upside down in confusion. I asked God, 'Why bring the love of my life to me now, just before I give myself to you for four months entirely?'

The words from the first paragraph of my testimony explain how I was feeling half-way through the four months in Patagonia.

In the midst of my feelings of being lost, confused and this 'missed-place' love, God came to me once again with a fourth grace, that of trust. I reached the most honest moment of my life where I was able to say, 'God I surrender everything to you', and 'be it done according to your Word' (Lk 1:38). It was in reaching this place of utter abandonment of my own will that I began to see the experience in Patagonia in a new light. I reached the conclusion that, 'If I am hurting this bad for leaving the things I love in this earthly world, just how much greater is the pain I will experience if I leave the things I love of the Heavenly world?' Through this time these words served me:

> 'Whoever wholeheartedly serves God will be accepted,
> his petitions will carry to the clouds.' (Si 35: 16)

For me, these graces of trust and love became the sum of community life. If you believe Christ is present 'where two or more meet' (Mt 18:20) in His name, community becomes a real living encounter with God that I have to believe in. It is the community that challenges and tests me in the graces of God: 'Do you really trust me George? Do you really love me George?'; they are willing to correct me of any misconceptions.

This acknowledgement of the role of community in my life has culminated in a clear direction for my life today: firstly, to work to build and share the experience of God's love (not just outwardly but also internally); secondly, to bring the graces I received to others through community, friendship and prayer (Lectio Divina). While these two missions can seem daunting (particularly in a secular world of life and work) I believe a fifth grace is being offered to me: humility. Humility is a continual encouragement to return to God through the removal of my self-will and earthly desires – and this is the hardest part of my journey thus far.

> 'It was good for me that I had to suffer, the better to learn your judgments. The Law you have uttered is more precious to me than all the wealth in the world.'
> (Ps 119:71-72)

For the time being, God provides me with a clear expression of support on this journey through material help in the form of the continual work with the Weave, my constant personal commitment to Manquehue (at times expressed through a 'Promise' of stability, obedience and conversatio morum), and a relentless pursuit of prayer and spiritual friendship. Amen.

'NOT WHAT I WANT
BUT WHAT YOU WANT'

Dame Andrea Savage
Stanbrook Abbey

When I look back at the tapestry of my own life, I see many moments when God had shown me a specific direction; for example, when I entered the monastery of Stanbrook Abbey back in January 1985. I felt I was listening to the promptings of the Holy Spirit, but I must admit I now realised that, when I stepped through the door, it was not with the full-hearted commitment I thought I was making. What I did unconsciously was secure my safety-net if things did not work out. God was given a year and, if it wasn't right, I was going home. Monastic life began with my agenda, but all that was to change over the next eighteen months. God altered my plans and made them rightly His.

Despite having this unspoken agenda upon entering, I nevertheless spent those first twelve months entering fully into the life of a Benedictine nun – first as a postulant, then, upon receiving the habit after six months, as a novice. It was a honeymoon period. There were times of great highs and then other times that were challenging, but overall, I was extremely happy. I found myself entering totally into life. Grace was at work; the Lord was attuning the ear of my heart to listen to His voice, showing me the way of life. For the first time in my life, I felt truly alive, and just maybe, that I was actually called to the monastic life.

Things began to change during my second Lent at Stanbrook. The Lord knew I was becoming too comfortable and was probably in danger of becoming complacent. It was time to pull the rug from under my feet. Life changed on Ash Wednesday when I managed to strain the top of my back muscles while working in the garden. I didn't discover this until the middle of Holy Week. The intervening weeks were horrible, as I became weaker and weaker. God was using this Lent to teach me a vital lesson born of the whole Paschal Mystery, and that was to let go and trust him. It was a tough, and at times, painful lesson to learn. The scripture passage from Philippians 2, which resonates in the Church over the whole of Lent and particularly during Passiontide, was ringing in my ears and heart.

> 'Let the same mind be in you that was in Christ Jesus, who, though he was in the form of God, did not regard equality with God as something to be exploited, but emptied himself, taking the form of a slave, being born in human likeness. And being found in human form, he humbled himself and became

obedient to the point of death— even death on a
cross.' (Ph 2:5-8)

I was empty and felt I was dying. It was scary. The Lord
was taking me by the hand and revealing to me what it was
truly like to take up my cross and to follow Jesus Christ. Over
these weeks leading up to Easter, there were many questions
I had to face. It was my will versus God's will. Did I genuinely
seek life? Could I become obedient to the point of death?
Spiritually, I felt I had fallen into a bottomless pit and was
scrabbling to get out, and each time I reached the top of the
pit, I fell back deeper into an abyss.

Over the months since I entered the community, without
realising it, I had become steeped in the Scriptures and the
Rule of St Benedict. As part of our studies, all novices learn
the Rule by heart. Each week I would learn a section and
recite it to the novice mistress. I found many of these verses
returning to me during these weeks of darkness, especially
the fourth degree of humility and the phrase: 'Anyone who
perseveres to the end will be saved.' (Mt 10:22 & RB 4:36)

In the middle of Holy Week, the crisis came to a head, and
I panicked. Physically I was struggling, and was therefore sent
to see the doctor. At last, she found the root cause of my
problems and treated it accordingly. Meanwhile, I was a wreck
inside. I thought I would be asked to go home because I was
unable to live the life. The real question was: Did I want to
leave?

On Maundy Thursday evening after the Mass of the Lord's
Supper, the Blessed Sacrament was taken to the Altar of

Repose in our Holy Thorn Chapel. My novice Mistress had permitted me to watch only for a short time. I sat there in the dark, and I found myself in the Garden of Gethsemane with Jesus and the disciples. In my head, I was replaying all the events of the past weeks, and the question was, could I, with Jesus, be obedient to the Father's will? 'Abba, Father, for you all things are possible; remove this cup from me; yet, not what I want, but what you want.' (Mk 14:36) As I prayed these words, I felt an emphasis in my heart on the words, not what I want, but what you want. Should I go and ask my novice mistress for my suitcases and go? At this point, I was ready to cave in. Was I, like the disciples, filled with fear at the sight of the soldiers, preparing myself to flee? 'All of them deserted him and fled'. (Mark 14:50) At that moment, I felt as though the Lord was asking me: Are you going to abandon me also? It was as though something had pierced through the dark cloud of my indecision. I knew then I did not want to leave but wanted very much to stay.

The next day, Good Friday, I went to see my novice mistress after the three o'clock service. I told her all my fears about being sent home, and I could not articulate just then how much I now wanted to stay. We prayed together, and she was able to say that any decision to leave at that point would be mine, but she did not think now was the right time to go. It was a turning point in my monastic vocation.

From this moment, I came to understand the power of the Paschal Mystery working in my own life. In life, there is the suffering of the cross, but I must empty myself of what leads me away from Christ. I must learn to let go and die to self so that 'I may know Christ and the power of Christ's resurrection working' in my life (Ph 3:10).

The emptying of Philippians 2 will continue all my life, but at the same time, it is not all death; there will always be resurrection moments when Christ's love will conquer all. It is the second part of St Paul's Hymn:

> 'Therefore God also highly exalted him and gave him the name that is above every name, so that at the name of Jesus every knee should bend, in heaven and on earth and under the earth, and every tongue should confess that Jesus Christ is Lord to the glory of God the Father.' (Ph 2:9-11)

I now try to live according to God's agenda always, in the light of the Paschal Mystery, and see this way of living as preparation for my final call to let go when the Lord finally calls me home. Everything that has gone before will be a preparation for this final moment when I can pray and say: Come Lord Jesus.

JESUS LOOKED STEADILY AT HIM AND WAS FILLED WITH LOVE FOR HIM'
(Mk 10:21)

James Moroney
Christ the King Community, Liverpool

I am thirty-one years old, a former student of Ampleforth who spent two years with the Manquehue Community in Chile before returning to my home town of Liverpool where I have mainly been teaching over the last years. I feel that I have had many experiences of God's love but was struggling to find something that I could talk much about. However, I experienced three connected moments a few years ago that I would like to recall as examples of being surprised by God.

The first moment was about five years ago when I was working at a school in Liverpool. One of my students, Mia, had a condition fairly similar to Down's syndrome but was still able to be in normal classes. She is a very joyful person and had a very good singing voice. Often in my science class, when something would go wrong, she would come up to me and say encouragingly 'Sir you are doing really well!' I also remember her singing a rendition of 'these are a few of a few of my favourite things' in an after-school music recital.

One day I had a free period and went to the school library to work. Mia was there with a teaching assistant, preparing for her religious studies exam. She was revising Mark's Gospel and reading out loud, rather slowly, but very clearly, the passage about the rich young man. Listening to her read, I felt that God was reminding me of my priorities and also reminding me that He wants to communicate with me, even in my normal activities and routine, if I am open to it and willing to listen to Him. Mark's Gospel has the unique and beautiful observation that 'Jesus looked steadily at the man and was filled with love for him' (Mk 10:21). I know that I can be very unsteady in my love, and I am struck by the consistency of Christ's love.

Later that same year, 2015, the Missionaries of Charity sisters invited me one Saturday to a little day retreat for their volunteers. The day was led by one of their priests, who, to be quite honest, spoke rather a lot and I can't remember what about!! But at some point, in the day, we split into groups. One of our group was a brother from Panama called Br Humberto. He was very small, dressed in simple grey clothes, with sandals that were rather large in proportion to his height; although about aged thirty at the time he looked much younger.

In our groups, we had to consider a number of questions. One of these was: 'Who is Jesus for you?' Everybody in the group spoke, with interesting and varied answers: A teacher, a friend, a brother… but Br Humberto was very quiet. At the end he spoke. His answer was: 'Everything'.

The day ended with a Mass and it was the 11th of July, St Benedict's day. The homilist described St Benedict as a young man restless for the truth. It felt that God was speaking through this and also reminding me of my connection with St Benedict at School and from my time in Chile. I also felt my faith was being challenged like the rich young man. Br Humberto and two other brothers stayed in Liverpool that summer and I was able to get to know them better as we worked together running a children's summer camp and homeless shelter. I felt very happy to have gotten to know Br Humberto especially, who gave a great example of humility. He clearly loved his family very much and had had a simple but stable office job in Panama before he started helping the sisters there and decided to become a brother. He was sent to study to be a priest in Rome and it was clearly not easy for him. When they left, I thought: 'I won't see Br Humberto again but I'm so glad I met him.'

The following year I was invited to go to the World Youth Day in Krakow with a group connected with the Benedictine schools and the Manquehue. I'm always a bit hesitant about signing up for unfamiliar things and was a bit doubtful I'd enjoy it but already had friends in Poland and thought it could be a very nice thing to visit them and then join the group after. In the end, however, the trip was an incredible experience of God's love. In the hospitality we received, in the places we visited and in the opportunity to be part of the group. There is too much to talk about from this time, but I will describe one event.

When we went to Krakow there were a number of public outdoor masses with Pope Francis and thousands of people. You were allocated a particular area to sit. The first of these masses it was pouring with rain. We all had brightly coloured folding waterproofs and trudged off to find our place on the wet grass in the sea of multicoloured pilgrims.

As we sat down, I noticed what looked like a bin-bag curled up about two meters in front of me. I looked more closely and realised the bag had a hand and rosary beads. It was Br Humberto… using a bin bag as a makeshift waterproof!! The chances that he was chosen to go to World Youth Day and that we should be sitting in the same place must have been absolutely miniscule. I was able to talk with Br Humberto and also deliver a letter from him to one of the sisters back in Liverpool.

For me this meeting was a beautiful example of God's amazing attention to detail and ability to surprise us if we are open to those surprises. It is difficult to say that I follow the example of Br Humberto or that I am always attentive to God's love, but I can return to these people and moments and many others as a gift from the Lord that encourages me in the present: an invitation to be more radical, loving and thankful. The fact that these meetings occurred through responding to the invitation of others but also to some extent as part of a natural working out of my particular responsibilities, routine and connections also reminds me of the value of stability and fidelity in little commitments. It reminded me that the Church is a global community and that Christ is present in all our relationships: sustaining friendships over time and through prayer. God connects us with each person we meet and even though we may never meet a person again we can be united in prayer. Sometimes we may meet at the most unexpected times and certainly in heaven. Last I heard Br Humberto was in South Africa. Probably he is now a priest.

> 'If I speed away on the wings of the dawn,
> If I dwell beyond the ocean,
> Even there your hand would be guiding me,
> Your right hand holding me fast' (Ps 139:9-10)

'I SHALL BE A WALL OF FIRE AROUND HER' (Zc 2:5)

Javiera Lubascher Díaz
Manquehue Apostolic Movement

'Jerusalem is surrounded by mountains and the Lord surrounds his people now and forever' (Ps 125:2)

I chose this verse to share my experience with God because it reflects how I feel God has been present in my life, how He has been reaching out to me and showing me His protection and love. Sometimes I have been able to notice it more clearly, other times less, but going through my path and history, I see that God has had me and keeps me surrounded by His loving arms, now and always, and that He has used many people to show me how He loves me, how He surrounds me with His love. I see that it has been necessary for Him to surround and protect me, because I recognise that many times doubts attack me and I tend to distrust God and His work with me; I know that I am rebellious and I fight against Him, but at the same time I can see that God multiplies His mercy with me, He has patience with me and He uses the precise means that He knows I need in order to reach my heart. Lectio divina, community and friendship have been key; the mountains through which God surrounds me, giving me proof of His faithfulness to me, waiting for me to trust Him more and more.

I believe that the first of the steps of trust were taken in the event of the death of a friend in my last year of school. I remember that faith, together with doubts, were very present during his illness and also in his last days. But I also remember very clearly that in spite of feeling great pain and sorrow, despite not understanding God, I still wanted to take the step of trust, and believe without understanding. Today I see that step was not thanks to my own determination, but taken through God, who has really always been there with me, taking care of me and helping my faith to grow. I had a teacher at the time who accompanied me, listened to me, and announced to me that God had a Word for me in all this, a loving Word that did not end in death. His friendship helped me to start looking for it and listening to it. Thus I came to know Lectio Divina, a place of prayer that has become sacred, because in it I can know who God is and how He is with me. His Word nourishes me, rescues me and opens my spiritual eyes so that I can see well: see reality illuminated with eternal life, raising my gaze above my human criteria.

God reached out to me, awakening my faith, and from there He has not ceased to make me seek Him. He gave me a way to be able to do it, and even more, a community with whom to share the search. I am part of the Manquehue

Apostolic Movement, which has given me the strongest and most beautiful experiences I have had of God. The San José Formation House in Patagonia, and my time as a member of St. Scholastica Community in Downside have marked my life forever. They have given me the gift of spiritual friendship, allowed me to taste the love of heaven through brotherly love. At Downside I discovered that God does not love me in the abstract, but concretely, through people: the community with whom I lived, the students of the lectio groups, the monks with whom we shared the Office, and so many other friends. God made me see that love leads me and opens up space for me to live eternal life today.

> Then, raising my eyes, I had a vision. There was a man with a measuring line in his hand. I asked him, 'Where are you going?' He said, 'To measure Jerusalem, to calculate her width and length.' And then, while the angel who was talking to me walked away, another angel came out to meet him. He said to him, 'Run, and tell that young man this, "Jerusalem is to remain unwalled, because of the great number of men and cattle inside. For I -- Yahweh declares -- shall be a wall of fire all round her and I shall be the Glory within her."' (Zc 2:5-9)

I love this reading, because I recognise how God has chosen to inhabit a space in me, and little by little, He has begun to gain more and more ground. He has taken me to different places to move forward, to let go and trust more; He has given me so many people who have become dear to me, some who are already in heaven and others whom I may never see again, but with whom I know that, in God's love, I have eternal friendships. And He does not stop; He leads me to go deeper and deeper; He has only shown me the beginning. He measures me, and widens the place of His dwelling, of His temple within me. Each time he urges me to give Him more and more space, with what that means at each moment: a path of humility and detachment, of letting go in order to love in freedom. And He announces to me: that place, God's sacred place within you, will be populated with many people, experiences, friends, who will take your heart and will lead you to live His eternal love more and more, to get to know this mystery more and more. I only have to give them room, so that His glory may grow within me, trusting that it is He Himself who keeps it protected by His wall.

A HUMBLING ENCOUNTER

Jonathan Stacey
The Weave of Manquehue Prayer

I really used to find prayer frustrating. I often asked God to reveal Himself to me and answer my questions with some great sign or in a miraculous manner: something immediate, direct, and free from any ambiguity. God however, wanted to show me how to live a happier life based on a radical trust in Him. Throughout my university years, my entire relationship with God has been one of learning to trust in His way over my own; learning to embrace the quiet assuredness of His love and let go of my ill-focused ambition and pride. To begin this journey though, I required quite a sharp wake-up call.

During my undergraduate studies, I had the opportunity to spend a year of my engineering degree studying abroad. Having spent my entire childhood growing up in rural Staffordshire, the prospect of travelling the world and experiencing life in another culture was pretty exciting, and the academic kudos attached to doing so would be a welcome ego boost! I was doing well in my degree – my assignments usually got the top grades – and so I had confidence (read here: arrogance) in my abilities. I was an ambitious young man with a habit of not focusing on the present, and instead enjoyed devising grand plans for my future academic life and career. In short, I was always most interested in finding the next thing that would make me look impressive or give me a competitive edge. To me the study abroad experience seemed like a fine trophy for my CV and fitted in my grand plans very well.

After applying, I was accepted onto a program at a very prestigious university in the United States. I was incredibly happy – everything was proceeding as planned; my CV would look great, and my ego was well-massaged. I saw it as something that I had orchestrated myself and would achieve entirely by my own abilities and ambition, and I began to allow myself to be proud of how I perceived I had made things. Now, I have been a practicing Catholic Christian all my life, and you have probably noticed that this pride and ambition I describe is not exactly very Christ-like. Indeed, in this story I have not mentioned God once yet! Reflecting on my first years at university I see a young man who, while still regularly practicing his faith, often put himself and his ambition in the place of God, and trusted in his own plans and desires, all the while figuring that God would just find a way to fit around him.

Reality struck in the summer before I was due to head to the US. Most of my examinations had gone well: second year was tough to be sure, but I had no doubt that I would achieve the overall grade required to be allowed to study abroad. The only other specific requirement was getting a good grade on my upcoming mathematics exam. Now, to say that the exam was difficult would be an understatement – there were whole chunks of the paper I didn't know how to answer, and the rest of the paper seemed to be made of questions far tougher than anything I had practiced! The bad news was confirmed a few weeks later. While on a semi-retreat, semi-holiday in Malta with friends from the university Catholic Society, I received my grades and the news that, while I had a good overall grade, I had fallen short on the mathematics paper by four marks. Four measly marks. I got email confirmation that my year abroad would not happen, and my grand plan lay in tatters. I was distraught and locked myself in my room, not speaking to anyone for most of the day.

I was angry with the exam, angry with myself, and especially angry with God. Didn't God want me to do well? Didn't He want me to succeed? Why would He bother helping me get so far with my plans if He would then let me fall at the final hurdle? After the immediate heat of my anger passed, I came to my senses and knew that it wasn't God at fault. For the first time in a while I began to think about what God wanted in all of this, but I couldn't really see how He wanted my sadness, or how this setback would serve Him. The more I thought about it, the more I began to think that I had simply failed God: He had given me this amazing opportunity, and I clearly hadn't worked hard enough and had ruined it. Was God angry with me? Did He even want to hear my prayers right now?

I felt quite alone, quite humiliated, and in no way pleasing to God. In the grand scheme of all the evils in this world, I knew I was upset over something minor, but I felt like I had failed God. In this dark moment of exhaustion, I simply asked Him to make sense of things, and immediately I felt peace. A quiet and certain peace.

After some time alone trying to pray, I decided to join my friends for a walk. They consoled me and helped me accept the reality of the situation. I would return to my university to complete my studies, but now I had nowhere to live for the new academic year which was fast approaching. Our University Chaplain had come with us to Malta (he organised the trip) and came and asked how I was. At this point he mentioned that he had one spare room remaining in the University Chaplaincy for the upcoming year, and it was mine if I wanted it. Simple as that. My hard-fought plans had collapsed, leaving me confused and angry, but before the dust could settle, I realised something better had been placed right in front of me. At that moment I finally appreciated that I was in a beautiful country, surrounded by close friends, and had been offered a lifeline that I felt like I didn't deserve. It became clear that God wanted me to be humbled – thank goodness, I needed it! – but not just to teach me a lesson, but to also give me something amazing, and open my eyes to His generous love.

The rest of that holiday was simply bliss. Malta is a stunning country normally, but when you're surrounded with good company and rekindle a loving relationship with God, the experience becomes something else entirely! Right then I began to suspect that God had put me on a new path, and as the next months and years passed, many wonderful and unpredictable things fell effortlessly into place directly as a result of this change of events. Only by being denied my study abroad did I get to live in the University Chaplaincy and meet amazing people who inspired me to deepen my faith. Only by being denied my study abroad did I get to later help lead the university Catholic Society. Only by being denied my study abroad did I end up doing research at the university that took me into my future PhD. Only by letting go of my own plans could I actually receive the gifts that God had in store for me.

I am reminded by a passage in the Gospel of Luke that resonated powerfully with my experience. In Luke 6:38, Christ says a 'full measure, pressed down, shaken together, and overflowing, will be poured into your lap', and when I read this four years after the events of Malta, I see the fullness of joy that God has had, and continues to have, in bestowing gifts upon me and guiding me along His plan for my life. For so long I had been obsessed with filling my own cup by my own efforts. God saw this and wanted to give me so many better things Himself, and encourage me to live life with a similar generosity.

Nowadays I find myself far more trusting of God. I still have loads to learn, but I feel absolutely no pressure to be or do any specific thing, because I know that if God wants something for me, He will provide it. My encounter with God and the subsequent journey with Him has been incredibly liberating, and I worry a lot less about where I am going in life, because I know I do not need to call the shots. In the past few years God has granted me opportunities and experiences that I couldn't have possibly imagined before, but it took a humbling encounter for me to truly see the Lord.

Old temptations sometimes raise their head, and the apparent silence of prayer can be daunting, but I now know these things pass. I really encourage everyone – no matter what stage of life you are in – to really sincerely ask God to show Himself to you. Ask God to help you see His plan for your life, and do not be unsettled by times of uncertainty or setback. Earnestly ask His Holy Spirit every day to show you any unnecessary things that you may cling to. Learn to let go of them piece by piece and put your trust in God and whatever gifts He has for you. You will receive far more than you can possibly imagine.

THE BURNING BUSH

Fr Peter Williams
Worth Abbey

In November of 1992, at the age of thirty-three, I was living in Brighton as a mature student studying for an HND in computer programming. Eighteen months earlier while travelling abroad I had had a spiritual awakening and had returned to the practise of my Catholic faith from which I had lapsed for most of my twenties. However after an initial sense of blessing, I was struggling with life generally; feeling that life had passed me by and I had not really succeeded at anything (in any aspect of my life). I was isolating and drinking too much and after a particularly rough weekend things seemed to reach a crunch point, I'd had enough. The following evening I did a review of my life, and tried to accept my life as it was, and the need to change and accept a different mind-set. That night as I lay in bed reflecting on this, I became aware of a figure in the room standing at the foot of my bed. Slowly the figure came closer to me and to my surprise I realised that the figure I was looking at was in fact 'me'. The figure seemed to be a younger version of me, it was dressed in black and had a striking simplicity and beauty. There then came a moment when I made eye contact with 'myself'; part of me was dreading this because instinctively I thought it would contain a judgement about me and all the things I'd been going through. To my amazement instead of that, I only felt a feeling of complete compassion and love enter me. The figure then moved even closer and merged into me and became one with me. From feeling very low and wretched about myself I now felt full of joy. This feeling of joy and excitement stayed with me for a number of days, during which I found it impossible to sleep and just felt like celebrating and literally dancing in the street.

This experience completely changed my life. It revealed to me that there was a spiritual side to me that I had been unaware of, that was more real than my physical self. Importantly, it re-connected me to my true self, a connection I had somehow lost on the journey of life. It also made me resolve never to lose this connection again. It seemed to me that this connection with my 'true/spiritual self' was the way I naturally connected with God. It made me want to search (with a single-minded purpose) for a way of deep prayer and/ or meditation. This search led me to the Christian Meditation movement and then on to monastic life – something I'd never intended to do, or had been even vaguely interested in up until this point!

During the years of my spiritual and monastic life since, the memory of this event has been for me a constant source of inspiration. I tend to think of it as my 'burning bush' experience, since it had introduced me to God in a way I did not expect, and in the process it gave me my vocation.

A number of years ago in the year dedicated to consecrated life, Pope Francis encouraged us to reflect on our call – what made us start this way of life in the first place – as a way of renewing our sense of vocation. The more I reflected on this and prayed about it, the realisation came to me, that in this sacred encounter, the one I had really encountered was not myself but Christ in the guise of me, just as He is present in the hearts' of everyone. What this made me go on to realise was that the saying, 'you must find Christ in the presence of everyone you meet', is not simply an encouragement to be more present to your neighbour, but is in fact a profoundly true statement. Christ is the presence at the centre of everyone – whether they know it or not. Sadly for most the realisation of this presence is deeply buried under a blanket of ignorance, fear, guilt and general wounded-ness. The work of the Christian and Christian faith is to release that presence so that it becomes conscious and in the process radiates light, love and joy into our world.

'THE UTTER FULLNESS OF GOD'
(Ep 3:19)

Rebecca Blakey
The Weave of Manquehue Prayer

'And you will know that I am Yahweh, when I open your graves and raise you from your graves, my people, and put my spirit in you, and you revive, and I resettle you on your own soil. Then you will know that I, Yahweh, have spoken and done this – declares the Lord Yahweh.' (Ezk 37:13-14)

I read these verses a week before having to book an early flight home to Scotland, my 'own soil', from Chile, as the onset of the coronavirus pandemic saw chaos and uncertainty erupt across the globe.

They speak to me now of the hand of God in my life. How I have seen the Lord, when He has opened my inner graves in these past years; how He brought me out of them, and continues to breathe new life into me.

Life new and life full: this is what God promises; this is what I have seen in those that have experienced His love and are living in His light. This is what I have desired with all my heart since seeing my first glimpses of eternity as a young child – I desire a full life, complete satisfaction, to live in the knowledge of the love of God; to share His joy and celebrate His goodness.

Always aware of my need to cling, albeit with an often-tenuous grasp, to God for the life I crave, I tried to make decisions that would keep me close to him: studying Theology, volunteering abroad with a religious community, getting a job at Worth School chaplaincy and, finally, joining the Manquehue mission at Downside.

It was probably this same desire for fulfilment which prompted me to seek life in all sorts of other things too: fun, excitement, travel, entertainment, good grades, and the attention and affirmation of others – all of them good, but things which, in themselves, can't begin to meet my immense neediness, my deep craving for peace, love and joy. More than that, over-dependence on such false gods has hurt me, unsettled my peace and increased my insecurities. A few years ago, the world around me, which had seemed so glorious as a child, began to appear increasingly chaotic and frightening. I started to feel desperate for security – becoming less tolerant of others and the world in general, but at the same time, feeling stuck in my own iniquities, growing in certain harmful tendencies, and hiding from the presence of God – all the while calling out desperately for Him to come and rescue me, to save me from the world and myself.

Well imagine that – a God who cares for a lost and silly, hurting girl enough to come and save her! Thankfully, the God of the Bible – of salvation history – is just that kind of God. He is the saviour! These past few years I have personally encountered the God of the Bible. The God who made a covenant with His people, rescued them from slavery and led them, with fire, out of Egypt into the Promised land. Who stayed faithful to the promises He made them, despite their betrayals, and patiently, painstakingly taught them how to see Him, hear Him, understand Him, and love Him. Who showed His love for them as a father, a teacher, a husband, a friend, and, finally as a suffering servant – who chose to die that they might have an absolutely full-to-the-brim life with him.

I have discovered my own place in this narrative in a special way these past two years since moving from Scotland, first to Worth, to be a 'forerunner' in the Chaplaincy, and then to live with the Manquehue community at Downside School. I have been spending the last two years, 'seeing the Lord', in life, Word, sacrament and community. The first way that God revealed Himself to me in this time was to show me that He sees me, and, in seeing me, loves me wholly.

A powerful 'revelation' moment took place when I first arrived at Worth, and had to attend a 72-hour worship festival. Upon entering the main tent, I felt the presence of God so strongly and terrifyingly, that I ran and hid in my own tent. I was very afraid of being seen by others, and by God – of

His and their accusing glares. However, it rained so much that I was forced to go back to the main tent and 'face God', and all I discovered was a very comforting and consoling presence, one that wanted to unburden me of my woes, and seemed to be saying, I didn't want you to get hurt.

A few weeks later, a boy praying with me felt prompted by the Spirit to share with me the verse of Jeremiah 29:11: 'For I know the plans that I have for you, says the Lord, plans to prosper you and not to hurt you, plans to give you hope and a future'. When the boy told me he felt God putting a specific emphasis on the words not to hurt you, I felt as though I had been hit on the head, punched by God, filled with certainty of His presence, and a sense of confirmation that he had indeed been with me all this time. Moreover, He really saw me, and saw what I needed better than I knew myself. It was like feeling the reassuring hand of a loving father on my shoulder, and elated, I spent the rest of the day jubilantly informing people, 'God spoke to me today!'

This time was one of rediscovering my identity as God's beloved: experiencing him as a father who desires my good and wishes to console me in my sufferings; and encountering him as a loving husband, who wants me to know that I am precious, desired, worth waiting for, worth forgiving, worth being adorned and celebrated as a beloved bride.

That year, on a retreat with the Manquehue community at Downside, we did a Lectio on John 1:43-51, in which Nathaniel, a cynical young man, recognises that Jesus is Lord when Jesus speaks to him with love and affirmation and tells him he has seen him 'under the fig tree' (vs 48). Yet Jesus goes on, after this exchange, to tell Nathaniel, you believe in me just because you know I have seen you and love you, but I am going to show you so much more than that: 'In all truth I tell you, you will see heaven open and the angels of God ascending and descending over the Son of man' (vs 51). Like He promised Nathaniel, I feel God has, since proving His love for me, been teaching me to believe that He not only sees my desires but wants to fulfil them in a way I could not imagine, more fully and more coherently, more meaningfully than I could ever have thought possible.

And by saying this, I do not mean fulfilment in the worldly sense of gaining a lot in this life, but that He is teaching me to find fulfilment in a life with him, 'giving me eyes to see, ears to hear, and a heart to understand' (Dt 29:4). He led me to a community, to the discovery of the great depth of meaning and life sourced in the Prayer of the Church and in Scripture, and to relationships that are schooling me in His love. Through all of these He has been teaching me, gently, to become more aware of my own iniquities, to love those around me more earnestly, to discover the path that leads to life and to follow it. Each day I feel Him encouraging me to step closer to the fullness of life with Him that I have always craved, which He has promised to each and every one of us:

> So that Christ may live in your hearts through faith, and then, planted in love and built on love, with all God's holy people you will have the strength to grasp the breadth and the length, the height and the depth.

So that, knowing the love of Christ, which is beyond knowledge, you may be filled with the utter fullness of God. (Ep 3:17-19)

'A LIGHT FOR MY PATH' (Ps 119:105)

Conal O'Callaghan
The Weave of Manquehue Prayer

When speaking of encounters with God I am blessed to say that I have a myriad of examples upon which I could draw. However in the act of writing about one I drew a blank. Personal encounters with God are, by their nature, personal. I looked through the catalogue I could recall and found many too hard to capture, articulate or convey to others after the fact.

I thought of my initial 'come to Jesus' moment at the age of nineteen, but found it too convoluted, with too many elements, and simply too hard to put on paper. If ever a movie were made on the subject, it would require a massive CGI budget.

I am left with one that was much the subtler, subtle enough that I was in danger of overlooking it. I also recount it, due to the fact that it is still fresh in my mind; not dimmed by the passage of time (and multiple rugby-related head injuries), or sentimentalised by over-analysis.

I found myself a few years past in the sleepy village of Walsingham, in the north of Norfolk, a somewhat ancient Shrine, dedicated to Our Lady, and a place of no little spiritual influence on me in my faith journey. I was staying there with a group of friends for a weekend retreat. As Norfolk is near to nowhere, most people were worn out by the combination of a long drive, a late arrival and a taxing week, and opted for an early bedtime. I, however, over-stimulated by a combination of the excitement of being out of London, and a little too much caffeine, decided to embark on a midnight jaunt before retiring to bed.

Given the tiny size of the town, I realised that to have a walk of any worth I would have to venture outside the confines of the village's diminutive limits, and into the open countryside beyond. I started down the old pilgrim trail known as the Holy Mile, along a meandering, hedge-lined, country road. In defiance of a lifetime of bad habit, I came, for once, prepared. Armed with a little pocket-torch, I set out into the darkness ahead.

After no less than five minutes of walking I had passed the last house lights of the village and was plunged into the darkness of the surrounding fields and countryside, with only the paltry light of the little torch to give me comfort. What I had imagined in my head to be a serene and peaceful walk became, in short order, trudging along a winding country lane in the enveloping blackness, with my head peering down at the road, trying to avoid being swallowed up in a stray pothole or tripping over a dead branch. Every few minutes I found myself being startled by the sound of a crunched leaf or the rustling of branches – only for my dim light to reveal a bemused sheep, a curious cow or a plump Norfolk pheasant staring back at me from the hedgerow.

Exasperated that the composed and tranquil walk I had envisioned in my mind was descending into a farce, I decided to collect my wits for a moment and opted to stay still for a few seconds and turn off the light of the torch.

Rather than being engulfed in darkness, I realised that I could in fact see much more now that the light of the torch had ceased; the path a hundred metres before me was now illuminated in a faint and mysterious glow. Although there was no moon to be seen that night, for the first time I looked upwards and saw that the midnight sky was bristling with a superfluity of brilliant stars, shining down to light the way. It dawned upon me that, although the torch lit the metre or two in front of me with an intense artificial light, it cast a shadow which blinded me from seeing any further beyond what was right beneath my feet. The absence of the torch allowed me a far greater field of view along the road, and the rest of my walk was quickly transformed from a perilous trudge to a tranquil and meditative stroll.

As I continued my walk, instead of staring at the few visible square feet in front of me, I was able to hold my head back and take in the magnitude of the heavens above me. I tried to recall the last time I had actually seen the stars above and found that I could not. The rest of the walk I meditated on this fact. The stars, though so far away (the nearest a mere 25 trillion miles away), are also so imminently close, that we only need look up and see them. However, there is much that prevents us from doing so. I realised I had not seen the light of the stars for so long because I lived in London, where the sky is too polluted by the throb of man-made neon and the all-pervading glow of the street lamps, for us to be able to look up and see the stars looking back.

As I walked along, alone in my thoughts with the stars for my only companions, my soul could not help but be lifted from the creation to its creator; the sheer artistry of the beauty above could not but point to the rather talented artist behind that canvas. Philosophers often speak of the *via pulchritudinis,* the 'Way of Beauty', as a means to come to know God, and the sight above me did little to dissuade me that they were right. I had always been at home in nature but had never particularly been given to spiritualising it or linking it to any transcendent reality, relegating that role to the prerogative of hippies and artists. Yet in this moment I could not look at the stars and not see a world 'charged with the God's Grandeur'. (cf. Gerard Manley Hopkins, 'God's Grandeur'.)

My mind was drawn to a line from scripture, which also forms the lyrics of a popular Christian song (that I began to hum along the path): 'Your Word is a lamp unto my feet, a light for my path', (Ps 119:105). I thought of how often I missed God's light right in front of and above me, as I blindly tried to stumble along the paths of this life, seeking out my own way under the paltry light of my own devising. So often I struggled with the need to do things under my own volition, independent and self-determining, desiring not to have to rely on anyone but my own competence.

God's light is better than my own, though it is never invasive or blinding, and shines the brighter the less I rely on artificial means of plotting my course. It dawned on me the need to 'let go,' to allow God to be God, and trust in Him. I frequently only do that when I have no other recourse, as the last option, when all my own best effort has been exhausted and found wanting. Yet, fundamental to the Christian faith is the knowledge that God is a good Father, one who desires our best, our flourishing, who knows us better than we know ourselves.

My night time jaunt unleashed no great spiritual fireworks, no overwhelming change of emotional state, no damascene conversion. It did however, impart a dose of much needed wisdom, a quiet, but determined attitudinal shift, an incremental, but no insignificant course-adjustment toward a better path.

As I crawled into bed that night, my take-home was the resolve to stop and look up with greater frequency, to turn down my own little light and trust that a good God has a better solution to the problem than my own. I slept well that night.

A PILGRIM OF FRIENDSHIP

Raimundo Zunino Maomed
Manquehue Apostolic Movement

'By the grace of God I am a Christian man, by my actions a great sinner, and by calling a homeless wanderer of the humblest birth who roams from place to place. My worldly goods are a knapsack with some dried bread in it on my back, and in my breast-pocket a Bible. And that is all.' (*The Way of a Pilgrim*)

I think there is no better introduction for a testimony than these words, and I would like to introduce myself as someone who desires to match them. I am Raimundo (commonly known as Mumo), raised in Chicureo, near Santiago, Chile's capital. An old boy from Manquehue's school, San Anselmo, I have been a member of a lectio group since I was fifteen. I have been involved in many mission experiences – serving the poor, spreading the Gospel and running Lectio groups in England and the US. I consider friendship to be central to my life with God. I will try to express how this is so in the next few lines.

I remember perfectly my first encounter with the living God; it was the first time I received the Sacrament of Confession, at the age of nine. Immediately after doing penance I started feeling a light in my chest that filled me with joy. It only lasted for a day, but the memory of it will never leave me. Years later, when I received the Sacrament of Confirmation, I didn't feel the light I had felt nine years before, but one of my classmates, I remember, said a fire filled his chest. So I took it as God confirming to me: 'Mumo, sometimes you will not feel me or see me, but trust me, I am there acting. It is not just about you; I am in everyone, in everything". This encounter with God was an encounter with the Spirit's fire.

The kind of friendship I experienced in childhood, the noble and selfless friendship of children, was radically changed, or rather, perfected, when I entered a Lectio group with many of my classmates at the age of fifteen. We started meeting every week to eat, play, chat, and then – sometimes when our parents were already on their way to collect us – we prayed. Once we went together on a trip to the south of Chile. Roberto Quiroga, who was the brother of our Lectio leader, also came with us. He was an old boy from my school and had just come back from five months in San José, Manquehue's formation house in Patagonia. It was through him that I started to discover 'something else' about a Lectio group and friendship. He kept company with us, sharing jokes, talking and laughing. Once we were talking about the *Lord of the Rings*, and in a blink, he was telling me about his experience of community life. At that moment I understood what our community had been called to be since the beginning, something of which, until then, we had had no idea. After that trip, my friendships began to grow deeper, especially within my Lectio group. Service was beginning to have a place in our lives, and we started to serve together. That moved our friendship onto a new level. It was just the beginning.

Straight after leaving school I went to Portsmouth Abbey School in the United States for a two-month experience of mission and community life. It was hard to make contact with the students but the effort was worth it for the few which I did manage to befriend. Community life, however, was just amazing. Dealing together with the very cold weather, traveling around, being ignored by most of the students, trying to understand American football and, of course, praying together, I was able to drink deeply from my favourite elixir: spiritual friendship.

Back in Chile, I started philosophy at University. What a desert! I started feeling truly thirsty. After a year, I switched courses to winemaking (not linked with the elixir or the thirst I just mentioned!). I was still meeting with my Lectio group, and going to my school to organise retreats or 'Trabajos y Misiones'. In 2016, during a mission trip in which I was the leader, the fire of the Spirit burnt me completely. During that week I spoke of nothing but the love of God. I am not usually a very expressive person nor a skillful leader, and I had not prepared well either, but that week I really felt the Spirit was speaking through me. It was amazing.

Of course, that week was not lacking in spiritual friendship. Being in charge, I had the opportunity to talk with many, so I got a lot of this real and very special friendship that comes from the Spirit. That same thirst for friendship pushed me to go to Ampleforth Abbey, England, in 2017, with two other friends. We joined the Manquehue oblates there for a six-month mission and community experience. In this mission we felt strongly aware that we were following in the footsteps of many saints that have spread the Gospel to England over the centuries. Of all the spiritual friendships I made at this time, the ones that struck me the most were those I formed with these saints. Going to visit them in the places they had lived, some very mystical places, I met them in the land and in nature, and I felt their company throughout the mission. Most importantly, in all these encounters with people ('dead' or alive), I was meeting God. This experience was so strong that, when the three of us moved on to travel around Southern Europe before going back to Chile, our trip became a huge pilgrimage of prayer, from church to church, and from one holy place to another, instead of the fun and partying we had first envisioned.

However, back in Chile, winemaking and bikes took up most of my life and God was reduced to a small corner. I had no Lectio group anymore and after almost two years, the fire of the Spirit was gone from me; it was just ashes, and I had almost forgotten the taste of spiritual friendship.

During Easter 2019, the brother of one of my friends died in an accident, and I felt like the brother of my brother had died. The experience woke up my sense of the intense power of spiritual friendship, a friendship built for eternity. During that Easter Vigil, in a dark candlelit church, I listened to the words of the Easter proclamation: 'This is the night, when Christ broke the prison-bars of death and rose victorious from the underworld [...] This is the night of which it is written: The night shall be as bright as day, dazzling is the night for me, and full of gladness.' Upon hearing those words, a light switched back on in my head, or should I say in my heart?

I returned to England during the British summer, to meet and travel with the community of oblates again. I rekindled old spiritual friendships and made new ones. This trip with these people made me remember that I am a witness of the love that God has for me and that He has shown to me through friendship. I was re-inspired to try and remember every day that I am 'a pilgrim of friendship', *un peregrino de la amistad*, seeking to love everyone to the extreme that He loved us.

Following my desire to be a pilgrim, I pushed myself to go to Portsmouth Abbey School again in the winter of 2020, knowing all the toughness I would experience there. I was going to be in charge of five Chileans – some old classmates, others new friends. I am still unpacking the experience. I saw a school completely changed, full of spirit, and made many new spiritual friends. In many moments during my time there, however, I felt deep doubts about my faith, but, as Basil Hume says , doubts do not soften faith but just serve to sharpen it.

I encourage you to listen to everyone's testimonies. I think mine is the fruit of that: listening to others and getting to know people through the lens of how loved they feel by this living God. Friendship, spiritual friendship, is like a precious pearl. And HE is the best friend! 'I shall no longer call you servants, because a servant does not know his master's business, I call you friends, because I have made known to you everything I have learnt from my Father.' (Jn 15:15) You must believe we are among saints, and you and I can also be part of them.

'NOT SIMPLY AS A DUTY BUT GLADLY' (1 P 5:2)

Maria Coyle
Community of Saint Aelred

My name is Maria Coyle. I am forty-five, a wife, mother of three, a full-time teacher, and currently the leader of the Community of Saint Aelred. A dear cousin of mine introduced me to Lectio Divina when I was eighteen years old, as he returned to England after spending time with the Manquehue Apostolic Movement in Chile. The very uncomplicated trust and love He had found for Christ in scripture made a huge impression on me.

I am a naturally serious, duty-driven person. I studied philosophy and I like to ponder weighty issues. This has often led to me seeking to understand God with my intellect at the expense of encountering Him in my heart.

'Would you say then, that he who so lavishly sends the Spirit to you, and causes the miracles among you, is doing this through your practice of the Law or because you believed the message you heard?' (Ga 3:5). This is the Word I was given before writing this testimony. It gets to the heart of how God is transforming me over decades, to fear less about getting my response to Him wrong, and to be more trusting and joyful.

Throughout my twenties I met many individuals who had been directly or indirectly inspired by the Manquehue to seek God in Lectio Divina and in community. One chapter of that story was as an undergraduate in Oxford, meeting weekly at Saint Benet's Hall with my cousin and with a married couple living near to Oxford. Praying Vespers and doing shared Lectio with people who were so unguarded about their life of faith, including their difficulties, made the possibility of a genuine, living faith going into adulthood seem real. I had been brought up in the faith, but sharing such an intimate encounter with Christ was new to me. That experience gave me a desire for community and a sense that God wanted me to be part of something big and important. At the same time I was rather overwhelmed – I had an anxiety that I was like the rich young man in St Matthew's Gospel and would be too 'wealthy' to put God first (Mt 19:22).

Fast forward nearly fifteen years, to 2009, and the fire had gone out of my faith life. I had not managed to set up a school, or live in community, or live the kind of radical life I felt so on the brink of in my early twenties. I knew God was present in my marriage and my experiences of motherhood, but I had a nagging sense that my response to everything was disappointing to God. Then a moment of grace came whilst I was on a walk and had stopped to look out over a lake. I sensed as if I were being asked to say yes to Christ, but was not sure what it meant. I tried, with as much of myself as I could, to respond with a 'yes' and felt a deeper peace than I had in a long time. Twelve days later I had a visit from my Oxford friend asking whether I would still be interested in being part of a lay Benedictine community. Reading the gospel of the day later that evening was another intense experience of God: 'Whatever you ask in my name, I will do it' (Jn 14:13). It was a powerful reminder, addressed directly to me, that He answers prayers and fulfils His purpose in His own time. I had experienced again the energy of saying yes to God. This was my experience of the start of the Community of Saint Aelred.

This new chapter was again, full of deep experiences of spiritual friendship and profound encounters with Christ in scripture. There was much discernment undertaken and an abbot carefully prayed for and elected. We prayed in our little Lectio communities in different parts of the country and tried to come together as a full community when possible. Once again, weekly shared Lectio became the lifeblood of my faith and I was hopeful that just by being part of the Community of Saint Aelred, I could avoid disappointing God and be part of His important plan. As the months and years passed, we did rewarding works, such as working with young people returning from time spent with the Manquehue in Chile and running the children and teenagers' programme at the Triduum at Ampleforth; however I still harboured an anxiety of not having achieved enough. The Community of Saint Aelred had not grown as we expected, and then when it was time to elect an abbot again, my friend said he would not be putting himself forward for re-election. I could not imagine the community continuing without his leadership and prayed about this. The reading I was given by the Holy Spirit that evening read: 'Give a shepherd's care to the flock of God that is entrusted to you: watch over it, not simply as a duty but gladly.' (1 Pt 5:2). I eagerly told my friend that I had a message for him from the Holy Spirit, but he suggested it could actually be for me. And so it was. Again, after another prayerful process, I was elected to lead the community.

I keep coming back to this scripture when the leadership of the community feels like a burden. I am slowly understanding that it is actually easy to give myself to God. I keep making the mistake of trying to measure the success of my relationship with God by outcomes that I have come up with. I am called to be part of an important work, indeed, the most important work, of growing closer to God, and sharing that with others. This goes so much better when I do it gladly, not just out of duty, and when I am responding to the message I believe, not trying to figure out the exact practices I am supposed to put in place.

One more moment in this story came some years ago after sharing my anxiety about disappointing God and being on the wrong path with a Chilean friend. Immediately after, we went to Eucharistic adoration and towards the end, I prayed and opened my Bible. 'Rejoice, exult with all your heart, daughter of Jerusalem! The Lord has repealed your sentence; he has turned your enemy away, The Lord is king among you, Israel, you have nothing more to fear' (Zp 3:14-15). It is hard to describe the weight that lifted off my heart in that encounter. For so long I had lived in fear of getting things wrong and this spoke to every fibre of my being that I was safe, and made for rejoicing.

I do not know what God has is store for me and my family, or the Community of Saint Aelred. I do know that each time I respond in faith to the message I have heard in my Lectio, beautiful things happen. I will always be duty-driven, but I pray that my tendency to fear getting my response wrong will not eclipse my ability to rejoice.

REBIRTH

Nick Majani

The Weave of Manquehue Prayer

Imagine experiencing a sudden unnatural feeling, which fills you with joy and happiness; a waterfall of tears starts running down your face; you feel as if you belong to something, that you are surrounded by a constant, loving presence, that there is a hidden reality which has been revealed. My name is Nicolas Majani. I am twenty-two years old and this is what I experienced on a late night six years ago at Ampleforth.

At the time, I was a student at Ampleforth College, a practicing Catholic and had already felt the existence of God in my life. Before going to Ampleforth, I was living in Martinique, a small French island in the Caribbean, and attending a local Catholic school. At some point in my childhood, I started being heavily bullied, and to avoid being humiliated, being hit, being seen alone, I would take refuge in the school's chapel dedicated to Our Lady. The chapel was rarely used – the paint must have been the same for the last sixty years – and pigeons and bats had happily made it their home. At the back of it, above the altar was a very big statue of Our Lady, which seemed the only thing that had not aged with time. Every breaktime, I would rush from my classroom and sneak into the chapel, which was probably out-of-bounds. I felt that God was my true refuge, Mary my counsellor, and both of them my heavenly friends.

Then I went to Ampleforth College. I was technically out of danger and did not feel the need to turn to God, whereupon, He chose to manifest Himself to me in a new way. One night, alone in my room, God revealed His presence to me in the powerful, life-changing way that I described in the beginning of this testimony. This mystical experience of God's love that I had that night in my room at the boarding school repeated itself every day for a couple of weeks. It became clear to me then that there was no escape from His presence. So I turned to God more often. Through the Manquehue community resident at Ampleforth, I discovered the power of Lectio Divina, and through praying in this way with others, formed many spiritual friends.

After a gap year that I spent in Chile with the Manquehue movement, I went to university in Lille, France. I was tortured by my thoughts, which were not all heavenly. The awareness of being a sinner was growing stronger, as was my awareness of the true reality. These opposing thoughts entered into battle. My mind was filled with the noise of the fight. Mental wounds were created, and I felt I was losing control. These thoughts had been growing since the end of my time at

Ampleforth, where my strong encounter with God had been nurtured in community. So I left university, and decided to join the Manquehue community in England for a year, from where I am writing now.

I arrived in the community at the end of a long summer, and as soon as I landed, we all went to the Youth 2000 retreat in Walsingham, Norfolk. This a four-day Catholic festival, which provides a powerful opportunity for prayer and adoration. It became obvious to me here that I had to go to Confession; it was at least two years since I had last done so. God then manifested himself in a more fearsome way than the first time. My experience with the priest to whom I confessed was an experience in which I felt I was talking directly to God Himself. As soon as I said what I thought were my sins, the servant of the Lord asked me two questions regarding certain sins. I answered, confessing one sin that the priest probably heard every day, and he started to cry. Then he told me every single sin that I would never confess, with remarkable detail. I started to cry as much as him. He described what I was going through in my mind, and as my biological father would, told me off severely. Then I was told two things by the priest. He said 'go now, but be careful for you are now a baby'; then he made a prophecy that I would be filled with God's love soon.

I felt naked. Stripped off, like Adam and Eve, I had nowhere to hide. I feared the Lord, and truly understood what fearing the Lord meant. I went back to where the community was and one of the members looked at me and said, 'I don't know why, but you look like a baby'. Even to human eyes, I could not hide.

Now reaching the final night of the retreat, there was a special vigil in which it was proclaimed that the Holy Spirit would be invoked, to 'fill' us. When the speaker began describing the many different ways in which the Holy Spirit could act, I walked out of the tent, thinking it was a whole load of rubbish. I smoked a cigarette with a friend who thought the same. He went back inside before me, and when I entered the prayer tent, the Holy Spirit had already started its job. The Blessed Sacrament was on a big stand in the middle of the room. Priests, monks and lay people went around the room, laying on hands and praying over the people standing up. I joined, standing up, not far from my friend, a bit reluctant. I had my arms crossed, and stared at the floor, trying not to listen to all the people that were crying, shouting and laughing 'in the Spirit'. Then I looked at my friend, intending to catch his eye and give him a look to say, 'let's get out of here'. However, he had two people praying over him and was in tears. I realised that if he could be affected in this way then the same might happen to me. One person came, prayed over me, nothing. Another came, prayed over me, nothing. A third came, prayed, and said, 'the Lord has not finished His work'. I collapsed to the floor in tears, and was just caught by the man. It felt exactly the same as the first time that God showed me His love.

After this powerful moment of reconversion and healing, I am now feeling a bit less than a baby but not much more –

maybe five years old. Knowing more about God, about reality, I feel now that true reality has been made mine.

I would like to give thanks to the Lord for all His manifestations of His love, and for the people who bullied me, as they are now some of my best friends. I thank the Lord for all the hard moments in my life, because they brought me to turn back to Him.

'TO LIVE IS TO LOVE'

Fr Martin McGee
Worth Abbey

Growing up in Newport, Co. Mayo in the West of Ireland in the 1950/60s was to absorb faith as easily as the fields absorbed the plentiful showers of rain. Faith was a natural part of existence and Catholicism was practised by almost 100% of the farming community. My mother was a woman of strong faith though by no means uncritical of the clergy who reigned unchallenged. I absorbed this faith in the same way that I learnt to speak English, to walk and to run. It was part of learning to mature and to discover the secrets of existence.

A key experience in my religious awakening took place at secondary school, my 'conversion' experience, if it's not too grandiose a word. As a primary schoolboy I had often heard the word 'charity' being mentioned and understood it to mean the act of giving money to the poor. One Sunday morning in my first year at boarding school I heard a homily which explained St Paul's understanding of charity as patience, kindness etc., a way of living which tried to put other people first in the nitty-gritty of daily life. 'Love is patient and kind; it is not jealous or conceited or proud' (1 Co 13:4). My eyes were opened and I understood for the first time that this was what it meant to be a Christian. And I was given the grace to put some of my new insights into practice. So when, for example, I returned home for the holidays, I tried to be more attentive to my mother and when asked to run to the shops, I would do so without complaining (I hope my memory is not playing tricks on me!). I had made an important breakthrough in realising that Christianity is above all a way of life. It is in trying to live the Gospel way of life that we gradually penetrate more and more into the mysteries of the faith. St Augustine sums up this insight beautifully in the phrase, 'For us, to live is to love'. And this is why I have never been tempted to abandon the practice of the Christian faith because I know that love is at the heart of Christianity and that it is love which gives life its savour and fruitfulness.

I became a secondary school teacher of French in Dundalk, Co. Louth in Southern Ireland. I had felt an increasing attraction to the monastic way of life. In order to find some time for reflection, I decided to take a year off teaching and study at the University of Durham. As the year at Durham progressed I sensed that I would need to make up my mind about monastic life. If I returned to teaching in Ireland I knew that it would be very difficult to extricate myself and make a fresh start.

One Sunday evening I decided to attend evensong at a city church. To my surprise it wasn't evensong but some type of prayer meeting. During the service I suddenly decided to open the Bible at random and see if it would cast any light on my predicament. This was something which I had never done before. The edition contained both the Old and New Testaments and I opened it at Psalm 109. I started to read and thought to myself, 'This has nothing to say to me. It makes no sense at all.' And then my eyes came to the lines, 'You are a priest forever after the order of Melchizedek.' I was stunned and from that moment onwards I knew that I should give the monastic life a go. My dithering was over. Those words from Psalm 109, in a matter of seconds, had put paid to five years of uncertainty. As a young person I had realised that I wasn't really suited to the responsibilities of being a parish priest, nor did I admire the power which the priesthood wielded at that time in Ireland, a power which placed priests on a pedestal. Nor was I attracted to the often lonely existence of the typical parish priest. However, I hadn't ruled out the possibility of becoming a priest in a monastic setting where the regular round of prayer and community life would provide companionship and keep my feet firmly on the ground.

Shortly afterwards as I was passing the students union building in Durham I wandered in to find that a Christian Union meeting was taking place. There were some booklets and leaflets on a table in the foyer. One attracted my attention, a booklet by John White called *Guidance*. As there was no one around I put 50p on the table and took it. It appeared to have been written especially for me. All my doubts and worries about monastic life were addressed – issues of location and certainty. The takeaway message which I found in the booklet gave me great reassurance. In answering God's call mathematical certainty is not available. However, we can trust Him because God wants our happiness more than we want it ourselves. I've still got the booklet and the phrase isn't exactly as I remembered it but it goes as follows: 'Take courage, then, when you have a tough decision to make. Someone who cares deeply for you already knows what he wants you to do. He takes delight in having fellowship with you and wants the very circumstances you face to draw you closer to him' (p.19).

As St Paul makes clear in his First Letter to the Corinthians, the whole point of the Christian life is to grow in our capacity to love, to become more like God. Love is at the heart of the Christian revelation and can be summed up in three words from the First Letter of St John, 'God is love' (4:8). And it is through participating in this divine life, through being taken up into this divine outpouring of love that we begin to understand the meaning and purpose of our own lives.

A prayer by Br Roger of Taizé which I copied into a notebook a few weeks before my first visit to Worth Abbey in 1986 captures the point of it all: 'Jesus, Risen Lord, placing our confidence in you means living in the here and now, and nowhere else. Our past lies buried in the heart of God, and you have already taken care of our future. When everything urges us to leave you, you are present. You pray within us, poor and humble of heart. Ceaselessly you tell us: "My love for you will never pass away. And do you love me?" And we stammer our reply: "You know I love you. Perhaps not as I would like to, but I do love you."' (*A Heart That Trusts*, Journal 1979-81, London, Mowbray 1986, p.120.)

'KNOWING THAT I AM NOT ALONE'

Tommy
Worth School

During this lockdown period, Mass is being held online – broadcast over live streams on the internet. It is easy to think that because of this we aren't physically present with the Lord, as we are while in church. What I have found from celebrating Mass in this way though, is that, lacking the fulfilment of Christ's physical presence, I have been forced to listen much more attentively, and experience Mass by hearing the meaning in the words that are said. The readings, gospel and prayers have been standing out to me more. In a recent Mass, while hearing the sequence being read, a particular part of it stood out to me: 'Heal our wounds, our strength renew, on our dryness pour thy dew.' This description of God pouring His Spirit on us to cleanse us of our sin – through the image of dew and dryness – made it clear to me that the Holy Spirit is necessary for living a fulfilled life. Yet it was also an assurance of God's never-ending love for us, illustrated by the dew that is ever-present in the morning.

This is one of a number of occasions in which the words said in the Mass or the priest's own words have had an impact on me. Often, simply the way a priest words a sentence has opened my eyes to discover a new truth about God and His relationship to me. I once remember a priest describing the taking of the Eucharist as receiving Jesus directly into our bodies. This brought me to a hugely uplifting realisation that Jesus is physically one with me after I consume the host. In my life before coming to Worth, I didn't have much understanding about the Mass, and so the words said didn't have the same impact on me as they do now. Attending church was a weekly event that I had to do, regardless of whether I enjoyed it or not. Since coming to Worth however, the way I experience the Mass has changed. I now understand the mass as a door to Christ, as each time we attend it, we are experiencing the Last Supper again and remembering the sacrifice He made for us.

Reflecting on my time at Worth so far, one of the most important (although seemingly small) events that helped me on my journey of faith, was being invited to join Nazareth* by one of the Forerunners around the start of Year 9. All it took was a simple question: would you like to join us for Nazareth this evening? But it provided me with a stepping-stone on my journey. It helped me to become involved in the chaplaincy and get to know the guest speakers who had spoken at Wednesday worship* each week during the meal we shared together. Attending Nazareth also meant I spent time with both Forerunners and fellow pupils. One thing that I saw in all the people around me in that community was their happiness and joy. This was something that I wanted to experience in my life.

Through these years at Worth I have experienced the happiness and joy of faith that I saw in those other people, and I think that being a part of a community has greatly helped me to do so. Knowing that I am not alone in the search for God has been encouraging and given me confidence. Yet being part of a community has also helped me to realise that faith is a personal thing, that all members of the community are on their own personal journeys with God, and that I cannot compare my own with theirs.

One place where I particularly experienced the beauty and strength of community was at a retreat centre in Scotland, which I visited with Worth at the start of Year 11. Every member at the centre had that same happiness and joy that I had previously seen in others at Nazareth. Their community was bound together by the love they had for one another, a love that God had instilled into their lives. Hearing the testimonies of some of the community members inspired me and made me acknowledge the power and working of the Holy Spirit. I was particularly struck by how the Spirit had acted through them during times of hardship or anxiety.

One of the many things I have learned in all of these experiences – listening to the priest in Mass, being part of the Nazareth community, and attending that retreat – is the enormous impact that one person sharing their faith with another can have. I continue to be motivated to find God because of the impact that these people have had on my life. It has also encouraged me to believe that, by finding God, I too can be guided by the Holy Spirit and share my own testimony to inspire others.

*Nazareth: after-school student discipleship group
**Wednesday Worship: Weekly whole-school liturgy

'I WILL HEAL ALL THAT THEY HAVE
DONE AND LOVE THEM FREELY'
(Ho 14:4)

Vicky Firth
The Weave of Manquehue Prayer

The encounter with God I would like to write about happened last week on the day before Pentecost.

I had arrived at Downside to stay with my dear friend Charlotte the evening before. I was running away from a stressful lockdown situation in Essex, and from an increasing feeling of anxiety and sense of separation from everyone. Even though I had been talking to my nearest and dearest more than ever, I felt strung out – the seemingly never-ending stream of video calls brought forth in me a constant worry about my appearance, which morphed into fears about people's opinions of me. I knew that I was meant to feel loved by God, but I felt that if there was love for me, it would surely be a pitying sort of love, rather than anything else. There is no hope for me, I thought. I went to Downside not so much thinking this would be a chance to reconnect with God, but instead went thinking that it would be an opportunity to hide from the world and my fears, a way to remove myself from everything and everyone.

Thankfully, I was very wrong and Charlotte had better ideas! Instead, I was launched straight away into a Pentecost retreat the morning after my arrival, one I had been signed up for without knowing, and spent the morning talking and sharing with friends over Zoom. I was doing what I had wanted to run away from.

But instead of feeling overwhelmed, I felt at peace. I had already witnessed the miraculous timing of a letter from Mary, who was also a part of the community here at St Benedict's, on Friday night, which arrived at the Convent Flat, just minutes after my own arrival, in the hands of one of the Downside monks. Wow, I thought. God's timing is truly wonderful, and maybe I'm really meant to be here. The letter was a welcome to Downside and a reminder to let God guide me and to not be afraid.

During the retreat, I was really inspired by the echoes that others shared. These were from friends old and new, friends I have seen many times and friends I have only seen once or twice before. The retreat was a mixture of personal work and sharing, including a 'Collatio' – a spiritual sharing on a common reading. Our text was from the Foundation of the Manquehue Apostolic Movement on the eve of Pentecost many years ago. 'This moment is historic', it began. Yes! For the eve of Pentecost this year, rather than the eve of Pentecost 1977, was to be a lightning bolt for me – a day which would ask me to rethink what I knew about Christian friendship.

That afternoon Charlotte asked me if I had written this testimony yet. I hadn't, so I went into the parish church to pray before starting my testimony (for clarity, the Convent Flat is above St Benedict's parish church. You can enter the church without leaving the building, so although it is closed, one can enter it from here without breaching the rules of the UK lockdown!).

I was desperately unsure about what I wanted to write about to share with you all. I had felt for so long that I was a mistake and not quite the creation God had intended. That feeling had just been starting to dislodge thanks to the retreat that morning, but I worried that maybe I had felt that way for so long that my eyes had been blind to my encounters with the Lord recently.

So, fearing thus, I flipped through my Bible and my journal, searching for inspiration. And so much came from it. Every reading I opened the Bible to, every reflection I read in my journal, spoke to what I had been battling with before coming here. I had been feeling alone and isolated and unworthy and friendless for so long, but here I was reading – in Scripture and my journal entries from the last five years – about how Jesus is my friend, and about the wonderful things friends have done for me and the hard times they have helped me through in the past.

Jesus is my friend. I was reading this constantly, in verse after verse and (from my journal) scrawl after scrawl. I was reawakening to the fact that, not only does God know me better than I know myself, but that He has also chosen to make Himself known and accessible to me. As my eyes were opening and my heart thawing and feeling the warmth of His love, it felt as if the church was ringing, humming, shaking. The air was electric and I knew that this was God really asking me to pay attention to everything I was experiencing in that moment. God is my friend. Jesus is my friend. The Holy Spirit is with me.

This truth has held me up this last week. I do not mean to say that all my worries and troubles have disappeared – even in the short space of a week I have had wobbles – but it has made everything seem more possible. Seeing Jesus as a friend has made a difference – I feel less guilt, feeling that I am just someone who needs saving. I feel that God wants to know me, wants to listen to me, wants me to confide in Him and share my struggles and trust Him to help me – just like any friend would.

I have seen the Lord, and remembered that I am not alone in bearing things. Jesus is there with me to carry these burdens: 'I can do all things through Christ who gives me strength'. (Ph 4:13)

This encounter with God has reminded me that the same is true of you, my friends, whether or not I have met you yet. Some of you have been through things with me, and some of you have helped me in your thoughts and prayers even though we haven't yet been introduced. I have reawakened to the knowledge that Christ lives in each of you, that he always has and always will. I am glorified in them, He says (Jn 17:10). Moving forward, I want to focus more on seeing

Christ in others, as I have been able to this week. I have also recommitted myself – with some prompting from friends beside me – to embracing Jesus as a friend in Contemplative Prayer.

> 'Contemplative prayer in my opinion is nothing else than a close sharing between friends'.
>
> St Teresa of Avila

'HE BROUGHT ME, LIKE HIS BROTHER, TO CHRIST'

Dame Petra Simpson
Stanbrook Abbey

All this happened nearly forty years ago, but is as real and alive as if it were yesterday. I was a teacher in a Catholic secondary school and we were gathered for morning assembly on the 30th of November, 1987, the Feast of St Andrew. My baptismal name is Andrea, the feminine of Andrew, so it was a special day for me, but my thoughts were really on the coming day's lessons and I remember having my books at my feet, ready for class. My father had died suddenly the previous Christmas and I had decided to move nearer to my mother after ten years of teaching in London. I found the school an exciting and challenging place to be and I'd decided I'd settle there and put down roots.

But everything was about to change. Assembly began with a reading from St John's Gospel. It was the famous passage in which Andrew and an unnamed disciple follow Jesus and he asks them, 'What do you seek?' When they answer, 'Rabbi, where are you staying?' he invites them to, 'Come and see'. Andrew then goes to his brother, Simon Peter, saying, 'We have found the Lord' and takes him to Jesus (Jn 1:35-42). The reading is deep and powerful, but it was in the words of the Headmistress, speaking about the passage, that I felt the Lord address me directly. She said that whenever we see Saint Andrew in the Gospels he is bringing others to Christ, and that he never gets in the way. This is our vocation also, she continued, to bring others to Christ, and not to get in the way. At those words I felt as if I had been struck in the heart. It was like a punch that took my breath away. I knew the word was meant for me but I could not understand it. It seemed to say that our lives must point to Christ and not to ourselves. But I knew it meant more than this. It would be three years before I fully understood.

It was the beginning of a journey and each stage was marked by an encounter which would be like a sign for me. I was thirty five and my faith was central to my life. I had been received into the Catholic Church when I was twenty one, being drawn by the teaching of the real presence in the Eucharist. I had always worked in Catholic schools , supported by a community of faith. Prayer was important to me, but at this time my prayer was really confined to saying prayers. This was the first major change. That spring I was asked to accompany a sixth form group on a three-day residential retreat given by a Benedictine monk. This was my first encounter with Benedictine spirituality and I felt instantly at home. Here was the first sign on my way. The retreat talks were simple and

Christ-centred. Between the talks I met with the monk and we talked about prayer. I told him about how the recitation of prayers had become dead and dry for me. I felt there were too many words. He said to me, 'My dear, you don't need to use words. All you need to do is to sit in silence with the Lord.' This was the beginning of a revolution in my life. Every day after this I went home from work and took the phone off the hook. Then I went to my room and prayed in silence for half an hour or so. This became life-giving for me; I felt as you do when you have been learning to swim and after struggling and spluttering suddenly allow the water to carry you.

About six months later came the second encounter. At morning coffee on a weekend retreat I met a lady wearing the medal of St Benedict. She said she was a Benedictine Oblate of Stanbrook Abbey and explained that to be an Oblate was to be in spiritual communion with a Benedictine community, sharing the life of prayer whilst living as a lay Christian in the world. My heart leapt as she spoke and I knew this was the spiritual path for me. Following this meeting, I discovered that Downside Abbey had a small Oblates' group and asked to join them. I travelled to Downside for Oblate meetings, began saying the Prayer of the Church and continued teaching, After a year's formation I made my Oblation, or 'self-offering', to God.

This was the setting for the next encounter. After my Oblation, a woman from the congregation came to congratulate me. She handed me a card printed at Stanbrook

Abbey and said, 'You really want to be a nun, don't you?' 'No',
I said, and I was very sure.

From that day, however, everything changed. I felt
increasingly that I was not where the Lord wanted me to be.
The teaching, which had been a great joy, lost its savour. I
experienced a time of darkness. We had a parish vocations
day and I said to the Lord, 'If this is what you want, then show
me.' One night, I decided I must ask for help from someone
spiritually wise. The headmistress always worked late and at
about eleven o'clock I knocked on the door and asked if I
could speak about something personal. Could it be possible
I had a vocation? We talked and she said, 'I think you have,
and it would be contemplative, wouldn't it?' That was a
breakthrough moment. It made complete sense, though,
strangely, contemplative life had never occurred to me. She
was down-to-earth and practical and told me I'd better get on
with it and not waste time!

As the only contemplative orders I knew about were the
Carmelites and Poor Clares, I went to the Benedictine monk
who had guided me in prayer, and complained: 'The only Order
I've ever felt at home in is the Benedictines. You're all monks.
There aren't any Benedictine nuns!' He roared with laughter
and answered, 'Oh yes, there are, my dear'. Then he explained
that Benedictine nuns are enclosed contemplatives who live a
life of prayer. He gave me the Benedictine Yearbook where
I found Stanbrook Abbey, the spiritual home of the Oblate
I'd met, and source of the prayer card at my Oblation. The
entry read very simply: 'Our life is centred on prayer and the

worship of God in community'. It was at that moment, almost three years after the assembly on the feast of St Andrew, that I understood the words that the Lord had spoken to me through my Headmistress: that our vocation is to bring others to God but not to get in the way. For me, this meant a contemplative vocation, meditating on the Scriptures and praying for the world night and day in the Divine Office.

It was not immediately plain-sailing. Very few people understand the contemplative life and many friends and colleagues thought I was wasting my life and my gifts as a teacher. Also, as you perhaps know from the Rule, Saint Benedict advises that any prospective new entrant is to be discouraged, to test their spirits. So it was with me. I was tested with waiting and it was only after eighteen months of persistence and patience that I entered on the 1st of November, 1987. I took the name Petra for St Peter and in recognition of St Andrew who had brought me, like his brother, to Christ.

The Prophet Isaiah speaks of the mystery of the Word. Like the rain and snow which water the earth and make it fruitful, 'So shall my word be that goes forth from my mouth; it shall not return to me void' (Is 55:11). This has been my experience. The Word has led me surely through prayer and the words of faithful Christians to find God in the life of community and my monastic vows. The Word takes flesh in those who love Him. He takes flesh anew every day in every faithful Christian soul and so renews the world. Trust in Him. He is always faithful.

FINDING MYSELF IN HIM

Elisabeth Lützenkirchen
The Weave of Manquehue Prayer

My name is Elisabeth Lützenkirchen, better known as Lisa. I attended Downside school from 2012 to 2014 (Sixth Form) and I was in Isabella House. In my two years there, I was part of a Lectio group introduced by the girls from the Manquehue Movement. In my second year, I became a Lectio leader for the third form girls. The same year, the Chileans gathered all the Lectio leaders into our own Lectio group: St. John's, which still exists today.

When I was asked to write a testimony on my experience with God, the moments that came to my mind straight away were the most spiritually intense moments of my life.

I have not always been as trusting in God as I am today. Especially when I was younger, going to mass and religious studies at school were boring to me. Only my time at Downside School made me start developing my faith and my religious views. It has been a great privilege for me to attend a school like Downside, embedded in a monastic community. I had not seen such a range of opportunities to discover one's faith before. I guess this variety of options made it very easy to let myself fall and to let it in, that is, to permit the possibility to (at least try and) meet God.

Nowadays, my life has changed a lot. Living in a big city, not knowing the people that I celebrate mass with in my local church, missing young people there that I can identify with, it has become a bit trickier to live my faith and see the Lord. And to be honest – sometimes my spirituality and the time that I would need for it gets drowned in other daily life activities.

The very first moment when I felt certain that I had just seen the Lord, was not a spectacular enlightenment. In a moment of decision, I prayed, I turned towards the Lord and asked Him for strength to make this decision. And on a normal school day at an early morning mass in the Old Chapel of Downside, I felt His support. It was not a burning bush or a parting sea. There was no old man with a grey beard sitting next to me – it was just a radiating warmth in my heart. I recognised a calm in my heart that I used to have when I was in my mother's arms when I was little: absolute security and no fear. It is still one of the most amazing and comforting feelings that I have ever experienced: listening inside myself and receiving a reaction this strong. After this event, I could say that Christ had been truly with me that day and He gave me a sign.

This moment changed my life. When defending the decision that I had made, I realised the confidence I suddenly had because to me, it was given by God. I was so overwhelmed that I had to tell my friend, a bit like Mary of Magdala, I guess. I had come to talk to Christ before: prior to exams, when I was homesick or when I was very grateful for something – in essential moments of my life. But now I felt like this experience of happiness had changed a part of my identity. Having someone to turn to, knowing that they are going to be there at any point in time, is reassuring. That is what we often seek in other people and I found it in Christ – inside myself!

I do not feel this same, radiating warmth every single time I pray. But I have seen the Lord once, and a few times after this first encounter. I still find myself, in difficult situations, without trust or in moments of frustration and stress where I simply cannot feel anything. It feels as if I do not have the energy to let my thoughts flow and to let Christ in. I have had to learn that I cannot force anything and that in these moments, I can still trust – God always solves these 'knots' in my head, but he does it in His own time.

I have always loved the phrase: 'For where two or three gather in my name, there am I with them.' (Mt 18:20) This is how I feel God in my daily life. I see Him in the people I love.

Thus, I do not exclusively mean having fun together. An honest conversation with understanding for each other, a moment of deep trust and care, that is when I feel that Christ is the link between us. This closeness can give you so much strength to 'tackle' life. When you can just love one another for who you are and the way you are. This is when Christ is with you – right in your midst. I have been blessed to experience this kind of friendship. It is a rare experience but it is very precious and it makes me want to share this feeling of being cared for with the people around me.

> 'And this commandment we have from God, that he who loves God loves also his brother' (1 Jn 4:21).

This phrase is the last part of a passage that has accompanied me ever since I have read it for the first time. Love your brothers to love God – it tells me that the love I give to my family and friends is one of the best ways to connect with Christ. And having understood this, I started opening up to the world around me, trying to have a smile for everyone and to treat them with warmth. I want to give back what I receive through Him.

The most special way of connecting that He has given to me is Lectio Divina. In my Lectio group, I saw the different facets and ways of Christ in my friends' echoes. Listening to them share their thoughts from deep within them, I discovered how He seems to adjust to every single one of us and helps us, if we let him into our hearts. This time of the week became my time to turn everything off, to shut the world out for a couple of hours and just concentrate on the words of the Lord, contemplate their meaning for my life. What does He want to tell me? What does He want for my life? This very practical way of getting in touch with Christ and each other means a lot to me. Sometimes I did not even realise what was deep inside of me until I read a word, a sentence, a passage in the bible, until I shared it with my friends and tried to put my thoughts into words.

It made me find out who I am.

I learned that listening to my friends' echoes was not only a means of deriving guidance. It was a call for me. As if He meant to say: 'Share so that you can support each other in finding your way.' Lectio gave us the opportunity to share these signs of the Lord with one another and it is a unique way of being friends – it is friendship in God.

I have seen the Lord. I have seen Him and I have had the chance to share this feeling. This feeling of being held, of being secure, this feeling of warmth and absolute happiness. It releases a gratefulness inside of me that I cannot describe and most importantly, it motivates me to go into the world and give this feeling to everyone even if it seems difficult or undoable at times. There is no test or criteria to fulfil, it is just about you. Who you are. It is love, and finding this inside yourself is a great gift that carries you – no matter where you are.

STEPPING INTO THE DIVINE DANCE

Josh Sharp

The Weave of Manquehue Prayer

I can't remember a time when God wasn't a part of my life. My parents are both faithful Christians that raised me in a home where God was very much a part of things. My father was (and still is) a clergyman in the Methodist Church, as his father was, and my mother helped run the Sunday school at our local church that I and my two sisters attended. My parents never forced me to go to church, but they encouraged me to, and I seem to remember that I always wanted to. I can remember one time when I requested to remain at home, and a reluctant father granted me permission. But I do remember a feeling of missing out on being part of something, being out of rhythm, without my grounding. Somehow I knew deep down that God loved me, and that He gave me a purpose in this life. As a family, we said grace before each meal and prayed together at every significant juncture of our lives. But it wasn't until leaving the family home and starting University that I came to ask myself: Am I really going to take God seriously? What kind of posture am I to hold towards Him? I was entering into a new world, becoming my own person, with no one around to be accountable to. It is safe to say that I did have a firm conviction that Christ was real and alive, but it is also safe to say that I did not have an urgency to follow Him. I was happy to welcome the distractions and folly that University culture had to offer.

I was delighted to be accepted into the University of St. Andrews in the autumn of 2013 to study Biology & Chemistry. I really did enjoy my years living and studying in this small Scottish town that was full of interesting people. I remember being a very excited fresher boarding the plane (yes, I flew to University), saying goodbye to a tearful Mum who was watching her first-born fledge the nest. I wasn't tearful though – I couldn't wait for all of what University had to offer. I loved the buzz of living in Halls, the comradery of the rowing team, the excitement of the nightlife! I remember loving the feeling of belonging, like I was part of something, a crowd, a gang. Academic study took a stoic back-seat; besides, grades didn't count for anything in year one. The other thing that took a back-seat though, was Church. I didn't seem to have much urgency in finding one. When the time eventually rolled around, a friend from Halls invited me to one of the local charismatic churches, 'Kingdom Vineyard'. I wasn't all that fussed about the style of worship or the sermon but I was drawn in when they plugged their popular 'Student homegroups'. The leader invited all new students to get stuck in with one, and so I jumped at the chance and went straight over to two homegroup leaders: Helen and Jon, who warmly welcomed me in. I'll never forget the journey that I went on through homegroup.

I was skeptical at first. I thought the praise & worship singing was a bit lame and over emotional, and the Bible-study intellectually below me. But, for some reason, I kept coming back. We were meeting in someone's home. It was warm, it was intentional, someone would take the time to prepare a delicious home-cooked meal. People were genuinely present, and they wanted to know me. These really were good friends, I thought. We all grew in friendship as the year progressed, and we began to share responsibilities of cooking, hosting, leading worship and Bible study. We all knew that we had a longing for community and brotherly love. I remember it being a stark contrast from the romantic and erotic love promoted so ferociously by the University nightlife culture. I knew deep down that I longed for more than that. I longed for genuine friendship. Jon and Helena were such wonderful hosts, and they reminded us that the joy and life that comes from being part of this group is because Jesus is at the centre. I began to realise that the community and friendship that I so longed for was most fully and truly found in Christ Jesus – who is a Community. An important book that helped in this journey is that of the *The Irresistible Revolution* by Shane Claiborne, who says:

> 'Community is what we are created for. We are made
> in the image of a God who is community, a plurality
> of oneness. When the first human was made, things

were not good until there were two, helping one
another. The biblical story is the story of community,
from beginning to end.'

Another significant part of my testimony is my introduction
to Lectio Divina. A good friend of mine, Ben, invited me to
the St. Andrews Catholic chaplaincy, affectionately known as
'Canmore' to share a meal and Lectio Divina together. I also
knew Charlotte from the Rowing team, who led this little
group in Lectio every week. I remember being drawn in by
the simplicity and solitude of Lectio. I was attracted to the
refreshing alternative of making space for silence, meditation
and listening. This approach was tricky at first. I was distracted
and I veered towards study, looking for an exegesis and
application in an attempt to show off 'what I knew'. But now
I have learnt that Lectio invites me to encounter the person
that is the Word of God. I am going beyond the word of the
page and entering into a conversation with the Lord. Lectio
Divina has helped me to develop genuine spiritual friendships.
In a mysterious way, I grow closer to my brothers and sisters
when we open our hearts to one another as we share an
echo from our Lord. Henry Drummond said that 'Sometimes
when uncertain of a voice from its very loudness, we catch
the missing syllable in the echo'. I catch a glimpse of what he
means when I hear something in the echo of a friend that I
may have missed in my own reading of the passage. Lectio
Divina helps me to listen. It wakes me up from my spiritual
sleep so that I can see the Lord.

I want to encourage you, the reader, to enter into community with the one who has been doing it from the start. The Father, Son and Holy Spirit have been in community since the beginning of time, and You and I are invited to step into this 'Divine Dance'. I am beginning to realise that this is the very thing I was created for. But that doesn't mean community is going to be easy. For everything in this world tries to pull us away from community, pushes us to choose independence over interdependence, to choose great things over small things, to choose going fast alone over going far together. It is tempting to go solo. But the Lord calls us – in fact He commands us – to be good friends to one another:

> 'As the Father has loved me, so have I loved you. Now remain in my love. If you keep my commands, you will remain in my love, just as I have kept my Father's commands and remain in his love. I have told you this so that my joy may be in you and that your joy may be complete. My command is this: Love each other as I have loved you. Greater love has no one than this: to lay down one's life for one's friends.' (Jn 15:9-13)

The spiritual accompaniment I have found in Homegroup and the Weave of Manquehue has helped me to step more fully into this magnificent mystery that is the Trinity. I believe I have seen the Lord. He invites me into relationship with Him and He invites you as well.

'THE WORD BECAME FLESH AND LIVED AMONG US' (Jn 1:14)

Frances Danaher
The Weave of Manquehue Prayer

My name is Frances Danaher, I am the third of five children and I grew up knowing God through the unconditional love that my family showed me. My parents have always been very involved with our parish and I went to Catholic state schools so my faith has always played a big part in my life. My parents always made an effort to engage us with our faith, for example by running a young Catholic discussion group for me, a couple of my friends and a couple of my brothers when I was a teenager where we could drink lots of random-flavoured teas and talk about things in the Catholic Church that bothered us and so by the time I was leaving home to go to university in Bristol, I felt well set-up to start taking responsibility for living out my faith of my own free will! At university, I became involved with the Catholic society (Cathsoc) at the university chaplaincy so I had a community I could share my faith with and I also had the opportunity to deepen in my faith through challenging conversations I had with my flatmates who were atheists and a Hindu. But one thing happened during university that had a huge impact on how I relate to God and continues to shape the way that I live out my faith today. This is the story of how I was introduced to a guy I like to call the Word of God.

One evening at the end of Mass at the chaplaincy during my first year of university, a group from Cathsoc got up to invite us to Lectio. They seemed super enthusiastic about the Bible and really emphasised what good friends they had become because of it. I wasn't really sure what they were going on about and kind of thought 'well that's lovely for them but 1) I'm not that enthusiastic and 2) I don't really think the Bible's for me'. So I went on with my university life and joined the Cathsoc committee as secretary. This meant that I was sending out an email every week to advertise everything that was going on at the chaplaincy, including Lectio, but I was never really interested in it myself. Then, as I seemingly wasn't paying enough attention to His hints, God intervened in a way he knew I wouldn't be able to resist!

At the start of my second year of university, as a member of the Cathsoc Committee, I was making a special effort to welcome the new first year students to the chaplaincy. So, one evening after Sunday Mass, I was chatting to a girl about all the activities we had going on in the chaplaincy that week. Even though I had never been to Lectio, I knew that it happened every Monday evening and so this was one of the things I mentioned. We continued the conversation and the girl seemed keen to get involved with Cathsoc's activities and so I was keen to make sure she was welcomed. So then at the end of our conversation, God played His killer move. At the time I didn't realise it, but now looking back, I can clearly see God smiling over us as the girl simply said, 'See you tomorrow then.' My heart sunk slightly – now I would have to go to Lectio! I couldn't let this new girl down. But of course then when I did turn up to Lectio the following evening, the girl wasn't there! Little did I know, this was a call for me and not for her.

So I turned up with some reluctance to that first Lectio and to be perfectly honest, I don't remember much about it, but there was something about the community there that made me want to come back the next week. And then the next week. And the next week. And before I knew it, Lectio had become an essential part of my week. I made really good friends and I started to realise that, not only was I wrong in thinking that the Bible 'wasn't really for me', but that God has a unique message in His Word, especially for me, which He reveals to me when I do Lectio. Through Lectio, I was getting to know God better, listening to Him and starting to understand how He calls me to live my life. And then towards the end of my final year of university, I received an invitation which again, revolutionised my story with God.

One of my friends who had been involved in starting the Lectio group in Bristol invited me to a Lectio Leaders' Workshop that was being run by the Weave of Manquehue Prayer, and with some gentle persistence from my friend and a general lack of excuses, I accepted. I remember being nervous on the drive there, thinking that my friends from my Lectio group were just going to meet up with some old friends and I'd just feel a bit out of place. Then, when I arrived, I was greeted with a huge smile and a massive hug from a girl I'd never met before! It was a lovely welcome but I thought it was a bit over-the-top, I just couldn't understand: 'Why would she be so happy to see me? It just seems a bit fake.' Then the next day, everything changed.

On the Saturday morning, we had a time for Lectio and it was my first experience of one particular method of Lectio: scrutinising. As I navigated my way through different parts of the Bible, I became very aware of God's presence with me and really felt God speaking directly to me in His question 'But you, who do you say I am?'(Mt 16:15). In that moment, I was suddenly struck by how Jesus is alive in everyone and as the time for Lectio came to an end, my eyes rushed over Peter's reply, 'You are the Christ, the Son of the living God.' (Mt 16:16). The living God. God is alive! And He is here with us now! I was filled with such an intense feeling of joy that I just could not stop smiling the whole weekend. I felt so light and free. I suddenly realised how genuine and perfect the welcome I had received the evening before was, because now I could see that it stemmed from this infinite joy and love I was now experiencing for myself. For the rest of the weekend I could not stop seeing God acting in every tiny detail. I would think, 'I haven't spoken to that person yet' and suddenly they would be coming up to me for a chat or I would read a passage from a book that made perfect sense of the experiences of

Lectio I had been having over the past two years. My eyes had been opened to God's living presence. I just felt like my life was completely in God's hands and He was taking such good care of me. Through Lectio, I had been able to come face-to-face with Jesus, the living Word of God, and it completely transformed how I saw the world and my relationships with the people around me.

Since that weekend, not only have I become more involved with the Weave of Manquehue Prayer – joining the Commission as the Communications Officer and going to live with the Manquehue community in Chile for six months last year – but I have also committed to giving myself time to do Lectio every day. To spend time in silence, listening to God, letting Him draw me towards Himself and waking me up to His living presence in my life. Sometimes I feel like I am really failing in my mission to follow God and hear Him constantly asking, 'Do you love me?' (Jn 21:17), calling me to share His love with those around me, but I continue to find strength in God's unconditional love for me – even though He knows all my failings and weaknesses, He still loves me completely, and exactly as I am. So, when I turn to God in Lectio and let myself be filled up with this perfect love, I can allow the outpouring of that love to overflow into all aspects of my life. Just like the sower who scatters seed over the field, God has planted His Word in my heart; 'Night and day, while I sleep, when I am awake, the seed is sprouting and growing; how, I do not know.' (Mk 4:27). So I encourage you to spend time with this Word that lives among us; 'stand firm in your faith and hope in the Gospel' (Col 1:23), because even though you may not see how the Word is acting in you, He is surely helping you grow up towards the Heavens. Trust in the Word, and He will lead you to eternal life.

'MAKING MYSELF AVAILABLE TO RECEIVE GOD'S LOVE'

Fr Richard ffield OSB
Ampleforth Abbey

I was brought up in a Catholic family, the third of four children. My elder sister joined the Poor Clares for a couple of years, both my Father and my elder and younger brothers had seriously considered joining the Monastery at Ampleforth, where we were fortunate enough to have been educated, and it was not uncommon for us to go to Mass during the week. I left school thinking of the monks as holy men and so not for me and went to university to read physics after a gap year during which I did an Outward Bound course and drove a potato delivery lorry to earn enough money to buy a car.

During my first term I found that university physics was nothing like the physics I'd enjoyed at school and that most of my friends were engineers. I thought about switching to engineering and asked various people for advice but as many people told me to stick with physics as told me to switch so that didn't help. How could I know for certain which was the correct decision to take, as it would change the direction of my life? One morning I walked into my tutor's office and asked if I could change to engineering. After a few questions, this was arranged.

Having caught up with the missed term's work, I took it too easy the following year and failed my second year exams. It took me three years to pass them on my fourth attempt and then I went back to do my third and last year having gained some valuable shop floor engineering experience. During this time I'd gone back to Ampleforth to run in an old boys athletics match and seen two or three monks whom I'd known in the school as perfectly ordinary types and began wondering if this was, after all, for me – or would I be just running away from failing exams? I knew I wanted to live a Christian life and didn't think I had the willpower to do it on my own. It was this or joining the Navy as an engineer. The experience of making a life-changing decision about my university course, without the support of certainty, was good experience for resolving this dilemma in prayer but without any blinding revelation. During an Easter Retreat at Ampleforth, I found myself asking Abbot Basil Hume if I could join the monastery.

He sent me to see Fr Bruno Donovan, the then Novice Master, who asked me what sort of prayer life I had. A prayer life sounded rather grand, so I said I didn't think I had one and he said I ought to get one before I joined in four months' time. It wasn't until years later that I realised that my regular Mass-going, my gabbled Our Fathers and Rosaries and frustrating repetitions of 'Jesus, I love you' had been, in fact, a living prayer life.

Not long after I had joined the Monastery, we had a Community Retreat from Fr John Main who told us about how he had come to learn meditation from an Indian Swami and that when, later, he became a monk he had been told he should use proper monastic prayer instead. It was still later, when studying Patristics, that he found that the fourth century monk, John Cassian, quoted by St Benedict in his Rule, recommended the same sort of prayer: silence, stillness, the continued repetition of a prayer word or mantra. I tried this for some weeks but it didn't seem to do anything for me and so I let it slip and reverted to spending my half hour of mental prayer vainly repeating, 'Oh God, I love you', without realising that this was actually very similar.

There followed about thirty very busy years of teaching, running the scouts, organizing expeditions and being a housemaster. I regarded the Divine Office as a necessary but rather boring part of being a monk and I kept pretty faithfully to my obligation to a daily half hour of mental prayer, but never found it very satisfying. Then I went to be part of our monastery in Zimbabwe and thought I ought to have another go at John Main. I read his three books and for the last seventeen years have been spending twenty or thirty minutes each morning and evening sitting still in silence, with my eyes closed and repeating the recommended mantra 'Maranatha'. It's an Aramaic word meaning 'Come, Lord Jesus'.

For several years I was confused and puzzled. Was this really prayer? I didn't seem to be conscious of God at all. Was there any point in it? What was the difference between what I was trying to do, rather unsuccessfully, and mindfulness or Transcendental Meditation? Most of the time I found myself thinking of all sorts of other things, even if I was still murmuring 'Maranatha, Maranatha' under my breath. I took advice from other Catholic meditators who assured me that the first twenty years were the hardest and so I kept on going. It has gradually become a non-negotiable part of my daily life.

Very gradually (no doubt with the help of the Holy Spirit), I began to accept that my distractions, including all my fantasies of which I was ashamed, really didn't matter. It wasn't that the mantra kept them away but that it served as an anchor to which I could easily return whenever I realised that I was miles away. I gradually began to accept that I wasn't doing the praying: all I was doing was to try and make myself available to receive God's love. I began to actually believe – to understand deeply – that His love really was unconditional and did not depend on how good I was or how much I was able to concentrate.

A brother monk remarked that he didn't think one could be really a Christian without having a deep personal relationship with Jesus. I didn't think I had that sort of relationship with Jesus. I did sometimes ask myself WWJD – What Would Jesus Do? – in certain situations and I avidly read books (such as J Pagola's Jesus: An Historical Approximation and the Dominican Albert Nolan's Jesus before Christianity) that sought to use the Gospels to understand how Jesus reacted and taught by example in the ordinary situations of daily life.

I think that the moment you are asking me to describe was when I found myself beginning each session of prayer / meditation with, 'I am your beloved son in whom you take delight', echoing – as we are surely entitled to as brothers of Jesus Christ – 'You are my Beloved Son, in whom I am well pleased' (Mk 1:11). As I continued to repeat this, day after day, I began to be conscious of being loved and supported. And, as it sounds rather presumptuous, I follow it with the Jesus Prayer: 'Lord Jesus Christ, Son of God, have mercy on me a sinner'.

The Cloud of Unknowing and other spiritual teachers such as Abbot John Chapman (whose Spiritual Letters I found very helpful and encouraging) tell us that the test of prayer is not how close we feel to Jesus or how holy we feel but that if we look back over the last month or two, during which time we have been faithful to our daily times of private prayer, we will find that, in some area of our life or other, we have become more generous, more tolerant, more kind – indeed, more Christlike. We by no means see this effect in all aspects of our life – it is a lifetime of growth – but with some particular person or in some particular situations. When we spend time with someone, we often unconsciously absorb some of his or her traits or attitudes. I like to think this is what has been happening to me. So that perhaps my 'wasting time with Jesus' hasn't been such a total waste of time after all.

'A SOURCE OF TRUE JOY AND HOPE'

Marcus Emmet
The Weave of Manquehue Prayer

Before the age of thirteen, I never considered faith as important, or as something that had any relevance to my life. I grew up in an ordinary Catholic family, going to mass on a weekly basis, but that was the extent of it for me. Every year my mother and grandmother ran a weekly first Holy Communion class that saw around eight or nine children receive the Sacrament at the end of it. I passed through, however I don't think they considered me a star pupil!

Everything changed for me when the circumstances of my life took an unexpected turn. In my final term of prep school, I suffered a series of retinal detachments in my right eye. Suddenly, from worrying about my poor batting average in cricket – I was now in a fight to keep the vision in my eye at all. Throughout that summer, I underwent numerous arduous operations. It was a difficult time for me. However, I don't look back at it with any particular resentment; in fact, in many ways I consider it a small blessing. This is because it was during this time that I truly discovered God and came to understand the intimate role that He played in my life.

The rehab from the operations were about a month each, spending fifty minutes of every hour lying on my side to ensure the gas within the eye was putting pressure on the correct area. The success of the operation was unknown until the end of the recovery period and I was helpless to affect the outcome. During these days I had a lot of time by myself… or so I thought! It was almost by chance that I discovered prayer on a deeply personal level, and thus formed a very close relationship with God. The experience was completely new to me, but my prayer felt very natural and I became at peace with the situation, knowing that I was loved intimately by God. My grandmother gave me a rosary which became my guide of prayer and, next to my bed, I had a small relic of Pope Pius XII with whom I prayed throughout my recovery. My relationship with God became so strong very quickly that I stopped praying for myself and instead I was praying for others, such was my confidence in the plan He had set out for me. Ultimately, the operations were unsuccessful, but this experience put me on a journey which I know I otherwise wouldn't have discovered.

In that September I joined Ampleforth School, full of beans and ready to embark on my new life up north. Indeed, I absolutely loved it and for three years, I got stuck into all the different aspects of school life, although I didn't manage to sort out my batting average. Over these years, my relationship with God continued to be cultivated under the guidance of the monks and teachers alike. However, in my GCSE year I suffered another detached retina, this time, however it was in my left eye – my only eye. Suddenly I was faced with the very real and probable possibility of total blindness.

I went through the same operation and rehab procedure; however, this time, I was truly helpless due to having no sight whatsoever, and unknowing if it would return. Again, I turned to God and I had no option but to trust in Him completely, which I did. I had such confidence in Him and His plan that I was able to let go and I never doubted that my sight would return; it truly was an amazing feeling of handing over all my fears into God loving hands. At the time, such was the strength I received from prayer, that I felt God's presence not only in prayer but at all times and it was a source of true joy and hope – like nothing I have experienced since. Gloriously, my sight returned, and I returned to Ampleforth for a couple more years.

During my time at Ampleforth, my faith was lived by going to mass on Sunday and occasionally attending Compline with friends. However, it was prayer through Lectio Divina that had a big impact on my life at that time. It was introduced to me by the visiting Chileans from the Manquehue community, who did a mission at the school and with whom I became very close. They invited me to come to Chile on my Gap Year. So I did. Myself and three others in my year at school spent six months working and living in the community of the Movimiento Apostólico Manquehue in Santiago, Chile. In this time, I worked in one of their schools, San Benito, and lived in a community of eight. Here my faith developed from something very personal to a faith that was lived in community.

Lectio Divina became an important pillar of prayer as I discovered that God was acting in my life constantly and was making Himself known to me in ways I was previously ignorant of – in every person I met, every conversation, every task and most clearly in the scriptures I read.

Just as important to me as Lectio, was living in community. I loved searching for God together rather than just by myself. Community life became of paramount importance as I was made aware of my personal and collective purpose. Community life presented many challenges; however the love and support of the other members far outweighed the grumbles I occasionally harboured.

After Chile, I went to Newcastle University, which I loved; however I didn't have the support of community, so over time I let the pressures of everyday life take over. At the end of uni, I was desperate to place God at the centre of my life again. I went back out to Chile for another six months. However, this time I went to live in the Movement's retreat house in Patagonia, where one lives a simple life rooted in prayer, community and work. In truth, I found it a difficult experience – nonetheless, I drew closer to God and it has given me the tools to continue to keep my faith alive whilst living and working in London.

My relationship with God is not perfect by any stretch of the imagination; I often find I forget the fundamental role that

God has in my life. However, although this may sometimes be the case, I return to prayer in confidence knowing that He is listening and His love for me will never fade. My faith gives my life the meaning and purpose I search for. Without it, my life feels ordinary and flat, like a black and white movie, conversely at times when I live my life with faith – my life is in full colour!

'YOUR LAWS WERE MY SONG IN A FOREIGN LAND' (Ps 118:54)

Charlotte Bonhoure
The Weave of Manquehue Prayer

I was sitting in the chapel of St Hilda, the women's house in San José, where the Manquehue Movement have their 'lay monastery' in Patagonia, to which they invite young people to live for four months at a time to receive formation. We were praying Midday Office, Tuesday, Week two. A verse from the psalm we were singing jumped out at me: 'Tus leyes eran mi canción en tierra extranjera' (or, as I translated it in my mind: 'your laws were my song in a foreign land') (Ps 118:54). I shed a tear of joy and a huge smile spread on my face because I knew this was a word from God for me in that moment. Here I was, miles from home in a foreign land, and yet content to sing God's praises. I understood 'law' as being love, which is God. I felt a renewed sense of peace, that this was where I was meant to be, that this is how I was meant to be praying, and that God was being very present to me.

That instant of prayer really stands out to me; it was a moment or revelation. I remember looking around at the other members of the community who had just sung the same line but the words hadn't quite struck them in the same way. Or at least, none of them seemed as moved as I was! It was just me and God sharing the connection.

In his Apostolic Exhortation to young people and the entire people of God, *Christus Vivit*, Pope Francis writes: 'The life that Jesus gives us is a love story, a life history that wants to blend with ours and sink roots in the soil of our own lives. ... The salvation that God offers us is an invitation to be part of a love story interwoven with our personal stories...' (Paragraph 252). This makes me think about the Resurrection of Christ, and how this fact changes my experience of so many events in my life, transforms them so that I can see in those moments how the Lord is loving me and looking after me. While I was in San José for four months, the Divine Office came alive to me in a way it never had before. I sometimes had moments of God's presence, as I described above, and I felt real joy to go to the chapel and pray with the community. I did not need to be persuaded!

I believe this transformation in my attitude to praying the Divine Office was a result of a 'Resurrection event' in my own life, which occurred only a few weeks after I arrived in Patagonia. The event was the death of my grandmother, on the 9th of September 2018. At the time, it seemed I was the furthest away I could ever be from home. I was surprised by how fast the news reached me: my mother (who at the time was working in Afghanistan) had emailed the head of St Hilda, who, having checked her messages that morning, drove me into town to find signal so I could talk to my mum. I learnt that my grandmother had had a stroke and was not going to live much longer. My mum was preparing to fly back to England to make arrangements for the funeral. I was full of thoughts that I should be going home too. The next day came the unsurprising news that my granny had passed away. The funeral was to be in two weeks' time, to allow for the internationally-dispersed family to gather at our family home in Kent. I had only arrived in San José about three weeks before that. My mum encouraged me to stay put, saying that I would be praying for them all from there.

I was very upset by the news. I was close to my grandmother because I had lived with her ever since I was fourteen. When I arrived in San José for my four months of formation in 2018, I remember describing to the community in detail how I had ended up going to Worth school for Sixth Form. I explained that my grandmother had suggested it as we drove home from my Confirmation retreat, which had taken place at Worth. The reason I was being confirmed at the usual age in my parish of fifteen, and very willingly, was because my grandmother had encouraged me to do my First Communion only the year before, and had found someone in the parish to prepare me. Before living with my grandparents in Kent, I had lived abroad with my parents and hadn't been able to attend Catholic mass regularly. So I was a bit behind on the sacraments! One of the girls in St Hilda pointed out that my grandmother must have been so important in passing on the faith to me. I had never really thought about her in that way.

To find out, only days after that conversation, that she was no longer in the world was a shock. I was particularly upset that I wouldn't be there to help prepare the mass readings, and maybe sing the psalm, especially because I seemed to think that I was the one in the family who really cared about those things. And I was the only one not going to be there. I felt very far away, and useless.

The day my granny died, we prayed the Office for the Dead. The psalms and the readings all spoke of the Resurrection and the life there is for us after death. I was able to make sense in a very personal way of what we had been taught about how the Liturgy of the Hours, the prayer of the Church, connects us to heaven, to all the angels and saints who are equally singing God's praises. Though they are no longer in a foreign land… I knew that my granny was on her way there; she was praying for me, I was praying for her. The Lord gave me the gift of peace. That's why we pray the Divine Office, to be constantly reminded of what it means to live: not that I am in the world, but that I have life in Christ.

> 'And now I commend you to God and to the word
> of his grace that has power to build you up and to
> give you your inheritance among all the sanctified.'
> (Ac 20:32)

> 'Let the Word of Christ, in all its richness, find a home
> in you. Teach each other and advise each other, in

all wisdom. With gratitude in your hearts sing psalms
and hymns and inspired songs to God.' (Col 3:16)

My experience of the Divine Office in San José, enlightened
by my grandmother's new life in Christ, has taught me to look
at life with the eyes of the Resurrection. I know that only God
can give meaning to the things I don't understand, the painful
situations, the mistakes I make. I have come to understand
how His Word, read in prayer, can transform me to make me
become who He created me to be and give me knowledge
of Him. It is He who gives me life, nothing else in this world.

'LORD, TO WHOM SHALL WE GO? YOU HAVE THE WORDS OF ETERNAL LIFE.' (Jn 6:68)

Catalina Cubillos Raab
Manquehue Apostolic Movement

My name is Catalina Cubillos and I am a recently married lawyer, who works in San Anselmo School as a formation assistant. I have seen the Lord through Lectio Divina, friendship and community; these three experiences have changed my life completely, and for them I am more than grateful.

I was born into a family that was Catholic but not very practicing. Every night, my mum would come to me and my younger sister's room to say prayers before bed. Thanks to her, God was a very present person in my life. However, my first school was secular; faith wasn't very important there. I do remember monthly masses, my first Bible, receiving confession and first communion, but clearly it was not something too significant for me.

When I was finishing 5th grade, my family moved to the suburban area of Chicureo, and because my school was too far from our new house, our parents enrolled us at the

Manquehue school, San Anselmo. This is not because they were involved with Manquehue, but because it was the school where my cousins were.

An important moment was my first day at San Anselmo when the entire class all began to say a prayer that I did not know, and then the teacher stood in the front and read from the Bible. After the reading, several classmates shared how something from it had 'struck them'. The whole experience was something very new for me, but now I realise it was the first time that I was facing something that would become hugely important in my life: Lectio Divina.

My life at San Anselmo was incredible: I joined the Scouts, tutoría – everything I could. There was something about these experiences that filled me; they were very different from the ones I had always done. In sixth-form, more opportunities were opened: Lectio Groups, 'Trabajos y Misiones', World Youth Day. I remember my first Trabajos trip as an experience that literally turned me around, made me want to give my life, give myself to the end for Jesus Christ. During that week, a reading spoke strongly to me of God's love, and I received a lot of tutoría from both students and alumni, and even from English monks. What I recollect the most from my experience at school was the number of people who gave up their time for me, took me out to talk, showed me different passages from Scripture, and witnessed to me of a God who was dying of love for me.

I became aware, upon finishing school, of how much my friends had influenced my search for God and my desire to participate as much as I could in Lectio, community or tutoría: with some I was in the Scouts and with others in a Lectio group, and participation in all of these have been key for my faith to grow. Without my friends I do not know if I would have persevered in all these groups and activities that in some way or another were evangelising me.

In the summer of 2013 I went with six others on mission to Ampleforth School in England. It was a difficult experience, but I remember discovering that God, as with the disciples walking to Emmaus, was walking beside me. However, I still felt that there was something more I was looking for: I felt I needed a criterion of life, a way of seeing things from another perspective. I felt I would find this in the Manquehue formation house of San José in Patagonia, and decided to head there the following year, to find what I was looking for.

I went to San José looking for criteria, training, wisdom; yet what I found was love, the most ardent love. God showed His unconditional love for me, as the Prophet Hosea showed to the woman who had responded to His love only with betrayal. I felt like that woman, with a hard heart, who responded to His love with treason every day, but I discovered that God's love is so great that He excuses everything: 'Love bears all things, believes all things, hopes all things, endures all things' (1 Co 13:7). In San José I discovered not only this love that God has for me, but also the love that exists in the community. It was a time for the Lord to speak to me, through His Word, through prayer, community, nature, work – many things. And I realised what the meaning of my life was: Jesus Christ is alive and, 'if we have died with Him, we will also live with Him' (2 Tm 2:11).

When I returned to Santiago, God already had plans to take me to another place. In 2015 I went back to England, this time to Downside School, to settle there, and to share tutoría and Lectio Divina. For me, this year there changed my life deep down. When I went to Patagonia, I felt an important change in my mindset; however, in Downside, I felt completely transformed. I had the opportunity to discover a path, a vocation. It was and still is such a great gift that I could never have asked for or imagined.

The community of five women were my home, family, friends, colleagues, sisters, and country. It was a very intense community life, and through struggling to live it, I learned to love. It's not that I've never loved, but I did learn how to do it. I had to re-found my relationships – that is, to discover that my true foundation is Christ and His love and make my relationships places where I can fully live love, forgiveness, and manifest the Lord; I want them to be spaces where I can express myself and be myself, because this type of relationship makes them eternal.

Also, I fell in love with England. I discovered that it is fertile land, a land full of saints and martyrs. All the blood spilled in these places has nourished many vocations and, in this world so secular today, many people still want to faithfully live the Gospel and cannot stop sharing this Good News that is the life of Christ.

I have been back in Santiago for almost five years. I finished university and got married. But during these years, God has given me many spaces to love and be loved, to keep me faithful to prayer and open the doors of my heart so that He can do His will. And in this sense, the reading with which I stayed after a year in Downside continues to resonate with me: 'Lord, to whom shall we go? You have the words of eternal life.' (Jn 6:68). Where can I go, where can I escape, if God has spoken to me during my twenty-six years with such force, and especially this last time? I have discovered that the Lord has given me a vocation to community, to Lectio and to tutoría, since it is in those spaces that I am deeply happy. In short, I have nowhere to go, nowhere to escape, because God has wanted to speak to me and change my life. He wants me to continue giving myself without measure, either in my marriage, in my work in San Anselmo, or with the people I encounter, because it is when I give myself up, when I love and let myself be loved, that I feel full. And for this, we know that tiredness, frustrations, or even fights are worth it, when we hear and share these words of eternal life.

RECEIVING CHRIST

Dom James Hood OSB
Downside Abbey

When my mother died in 1991, my father asked me to select two small texts for the memorial card. I had no difficulty in choosing the following: "He who eats my flesh and drinks my blood has eternal life, and I will raise him up at the last day" (Jn 6:54). The second text was from the Prologue of the Rule of St Benedict: "Whenever you begin to undertake any good work, beg Him with most earnest prayer to bring it to completion."

These two verses from St John's Gospel and the Rule of St Benedict are about the Eucharist, the Mass and prayer. As a child, my brother, two sisters and I were brought up in a family where the Mass and prayer were at the heart of our lives. It goes without saying that we never missed Sunday Mass and we often went to an early weekday Mass, especially if our grandmother was staying with us. On Sunday evenings we would kneel by the bed in my parents' bedroom to pray, saying a decade of the rosary and a prayer for the canonisation of the Forty Martyrs of England and Wales and for the Conversion of England to the true faith. From an early age Mass and prayer were at the heart of my life.

My prep school was St Philip's in London and I was moved by the masses we attended on the big feasts at the Brompton Oratory in South Kensington. In the late 1960s I came to Downside. During my time in the school, the Abbey Church was closed whilst the church was reordered. It was a time of experimental liturgy and a trying out of new ways of running retreats. Despite all these changes and experiments of the late 1960s and early 1970s three boys joined the monastic community, one joined the Worth community and there were three or four vocations to the secular priesthood. There must have been something that spoke to us. What?

The first thing for me was the Lourdes Pilgrimage I went on in 1968. As a very young boy, I saw a notice on a board inviting anyone who was interested in going to Lourdes to see Fr Laurence. On reading the notice, I felt a strong desire to go but I was too young. When I spoke to my parents they said my father would accompany me. It was a tiring, action-packed and very moving week. My heart was deeply touched as I helped push the sick around Lourdes, taking part in the afternoon procession of the Blessed Sacrament and the mass in the Grotto where the Blessed Virgin Mary had appeared to the young Bernadette Soubirous.

There were two retreats that touched me. One was given by a White Father – Fr Shanaghan. He was an inspiring speaker who knew how to communicate with the young. At another retreat I remember gathering in a small group to pray, reflecting quietly and meditatively on the Word of God; again the deep presence of God touched my heart.

Prayer and the Mass were at the centre of our life at home and we welcomed many friends. Among my parents' friends were priests and I admired each in his own way. They were all very different men but the common denominator was their love for God and their desire to pass on that love to others. Our parish church in London was the Carmelites in Church Street. The Friars seemed to exude holiness, kindness and a love for God; my heart was moved as they celebrated early morning Mass.

I think that it came as no surprise when I told family and friends that I wanted to join the Downside Community, and I did so a year after leaving school. In my early years at Downside I was to learn more about prayer. Dom Daniel Rees was my novice master and he passed on to us the love and richness of the monastic life with the importance of that daily personal communion with Jesus in prayer.

After Ordination to the Priesthood in June 1980, I started work in the school. It was a busy and tiring time. It was important to find time every day for quiet personal prayer and to join the brethren for the Conventual Mass and as many of the Offices I could make. The early 1990s were difficult years as my mother died in 1991 and my father in 1993. Not long before my father died my health broke down and I was left paralysed on the left side of my face with Bells' Palsy. Amidst this pain and desolation, it was difficult to pray, so I turned to saying the rosary that I had learnt as a boy.

After several busy years, I had the chance to spend some months in Santiago, Chile, with the Manquehue Apostolic Movement. At the heart of their spirituality is Lectio Divina, a prayerful and meditative reading of the scriptures. In his Rule, St Benedict envisages that the monk spend at least two or three hours every day in Lectio Divina, allowing the Word of God to touch his heart. My time with the Manquehue Movement was one of great joy, happiness and growth as I rediscovered this way of daily encounter with the Lord in the scriptures and, in doing so, rediscovered a way to prepare my heart for the encounter with the Lord in the celebration of Mass.

There are many things I could write about those months in Chile, but there is one particular story I'll recount. Every Thursday morning I used to visit and take Holy Communion to the poor, elderly and housebound parishioners around San Lorenzo School, a poor district in Santiago. On one occasion I was visiting a very elderly couple for the second or third time: she was in her nineties and he was nearly a hundred, very frail, blind and lying on his bed. I took communion to the elderly woman and then sat by the bed of the elderly man, praying and holding his hand. As I prayed with him, the old man's face suddenly lit up; for a short moment it was the most beautiful face I have ever seen; the light of Christ shone in those dark and tired eyes and touched my heart. That old, blind and deaf man lying on his bed that morning was passing on to me the

Light of Christ and I felt God telling me to bring that precious light to others.

The last fifteen years have been spent working as chaplain in the school, passing on to the young the love of God and encouraging them to have God at the centre of their lives. Since 2015, I have also been the novice master in the monastery, passing on the love of the monastic life to two novices. It is a privilege to have these responsibilities. I feel that I learn much from the young as the love of God that dwells in their hearts touches my heart.

Christ reveals himself to us all the time. We encounter a loving Christ when we receive the Sacraments. The Sacraments of Confession and Communion are moments of grace. In confession, we bring ourselves with all our faults and sins before Almighty God and He listens to us and gives us His healing love. 'When I think: "I have lost my foothold"; your mercy, Lord, holds me up. When cares increase in my heart your consolation calms my soul' (Ps 93:18-19). In Communion, Christ gives Himself to us in a unique way: He fills our heart and soul with His love. Let us open our hearts to that gift of love. Let us not be afraid to step out of time and shut out the noise, bustle and the hundred and one cares of the world so that God can reach us, so God can rest in our heart and we can then listen to Him.

'HE WELCOMED ME BACK INTO HIS HEART'

Emmanuelle Toone
Ampleforth College

My name is Emmanuelle Toone and I am twenty years old, studying Theatre and Performance at The University of Leeds. Before this, however, I was a student at Ampleforth College which provided the space that aided my faith to blossom. My father stayed with the Manquehue movement in Chile back in the late eighties and since then my brother has been and my younger sister is going next year.

Throughout my life, I have had a Catholic upbringing; going to mass every Sunday and praying every day. Before I was old enough to actually think about what faith was or who God was, it seemed normal and something that everybody did. I have now realised that it is definitely not the norm and not everyone does it. I believe that my faith is so strong not particularly because of reading the Bible but because of the people who have touched my lives with it and lived it with me. I get my energy off other people and there have been so many people in my life whose faith has made mine consolidate a firmer foundation.

As I mentioned previously, I have had a Catholic upbringing but there comes a point in your life when you make the decision to take your faith into your own hands and have to consciously make the effort to attend mass and live your faith in the way that you need to. However, this sounds easier than it is as going to university made this a huge hurdle to tackle. I attended the Manquehue's retreat at Douai Abbey at the beginning of June where I was speaking with a friend and she was comparing religion and faith to eating. She was saying that just as you need to cook for yourself at university, in the same way you need to take your faith into your own hands and live it yourself without any parents or figures of authority telling you to do so. This really resonated with me as she put it so simply, making me realise how simple and essential it was for me to practice my faith.

I feel as though my own spiritual journey pretty much started during my last year at school and is still very much developing. In amongst my A-levels in 2015, I experienced a lot of tragedies happening around me throughout which I needed God by my side. It was an extremely testing time for my family and for our close friends. Throughout this time, it would have been easy to blame God and feel as though God had let us all down. However, I have never felt the Holy Spirit so prevalently in my life since this point. It was a time that we were all in communion with Jesus, bearing our own crosses in the same way that He did. That year I also visited Lourdes for the

second time. By this point in the year, our close family friends'
three-year-old daughter had unexpectedly died, as well as my
Grandfather. My Grandmother was suffering a brain tumour
at this time as well. With all these things happening around
me, I went to Lourdes with a need for peace and reassurance,
pleading God to justify why all of this was happening. There
were a few moments in which I did feel this reassurance and
this came from experiencing Mary our Mother's intervention
in my life, at the grotto and in the Basilica. I had a very profound
experience in the Basilica which has provided so many fruits in
my life and in the lives of others.

Going from being surrounded by the Holy Spirit and people
who had the strongest faith that I have ever witnessed, into
a university environment where no one knew what had
happened to me in the prior months, was a huge shock that
shook me and as a result shook my faith, not in a good way.

Like anybody else, I enjoy having a good time and your first
year at university is probably the year that one is taken to
the extreme in this area: no responsibilities, a student loan
which no one is monitoring and a lot of free time. These three
things in combination can be a recipe for disaster if you like
enjoying yourself. If I'm being honest, my first year at university
unintentionally distanced me from God as I was surrounded
by a lot of people that didn't understand religion or why it
was important or, simply adamantly rejected it. From coming
into contact with these people, as lovely as they are and a
lot of them are my close friends, I started to question how
important attending mass was and how important praying

was. Before I knew it, I had missed mass over five times in a row and was substituting this time with having fun with friends, either drinking pimms in the sun or just simply wasting time. Saying all of this however, I knew in my heart that I was consciously disconnecting myself from Christ and ultimately distancing myself from what I knew was right – from what I knew was so very necessary in my life.

Throughout my first year at university, my parents kept mentioning to me that I must attend the World Youth Day (WYD) that was happening in July 2016. There was not a point that I felt particularly excited or motivated to go but something within me was telling me that I must go. I often get this feeling, and I think that I can only say that it is the Holy Spirit. The Holy Spirit that has been planted in every single one of us who is there to help us and keep us close to God. Before I could make a confirmed decision, my parents had booked my flights and, with some encouragement from some close friends and family, I went to Krakow (which is where WYD was).

I spent just short of two weeks living with two different Polish families and, in the back end of these ten days, I attended World Youth Day Krakow amongst a small group of Old Amplefordians, friends from other schools, my sister and members of the Ampleforth and Manquehue community. This week shook me back into place, reminding me and imprinting on me a stronger faith than I had ever had. In this time in Krakow, I was almost forced by the Holy Spirit to open my heart and accept the healing and forgiveness that God was so longing to give me. He welcomed me back into his heart with open arms and, once again, I felt God's immense love and overwhelming presence back in my life and, this time, I knew that it wasn't going to leave me again. From this experience in World Youth Day with so many inspiring young Catholics, I was inspired to form a Lectio Divina group back in my Catholic Chaplaincy in Leeds. We meet as often as we can and it has helped me keep my faith intact and remember God's all-loving attitude that we must all live in our lives.

I would say that my story should reassure those who maybe feel slightly weaker when practicing their faith especially whilst trying to balance an active social life at university. Even if you have committed what you think are unforgivable sins and you think that you have distanced yourself away from God, don't ever feel as though you cannot come back because He loves and accepts everyone. He knows that we sin but He wants to forgive and with God's forgiveness you can live in communion with Him.

N.B. I wrote this testimony over four years ago now and since then, God has taken me on such an adventure of healing and wonder through showing me His incredible goodness. The last four years have been rich with God pouring His generosity out on me and Him gently revealing more of Himself to me as I continue along my journey with Him, despite my struggles.

Every day, I try to choose God and, be assured, this was not the case when I wrote this testimony. I want to offer encouragement to anyone reading this who feels that a part of their heart (small or big) is far away from Jesus; you are never too far away from Him – He is right there waiting for you to invite Him into your heart. He has not given up on you and can work miracles in your life if you allow Him.

Our God is gentle and knows you better than you know yourself – all he needs is an invitation.

'MY BELOVED IS MINE AND I AM HIS'
(Sg 2:16)

Dame Philippa Edwards
Stanbrook Abbey

Perhaps my most dramatic encounter with the Lord was when He called me to follow Him in the monastic life. I was living in Rome, working as a nanny to two small Italian children, almost penniless, ignorant of the language, with just a handful of contacts in the city, when I attended Mass in English at the Irish Augustinian seminary. At this stage, over fifty years later, I'm not certain which passage of the Gospel was read at Mass but I heard loud and clear 'Leave everything and come, follow me' and I knew with absolute certainty that these words were directed at me.

And I said Yes. Of course it took quite a long time in the following weeks and months to work out the practical implications of this Yes, and to find the monastery which I eventually entered: Stanbrook in Worcester. But there is no doubt that it was on that occasion, the 6th of February, 1970, that I first encountered the power of the Word of God. This has often taken place in the context of the liturgy; and the liturgical cycle has had a profound effect upon me. I went into the Easter Vigil in that same 1970 convinced that the thought of becoming a nun was sheer masochism and by the time the Vigil was over my mind was made up in the opposite direction.

All the mile-stones of my monastic life have happened at Easter – clothing, simple profession and final profession. And the Paschal Mystery has become the central theme of my entire life.

Many years ago I read a tiny book: Personal Vocation by an Indian Jesuit, Herbie Alphonso. Its theme is that every human being has a personal individual call from God which can be encapsulated in a phrase from Scripture. I came to the conclusion that my particular phrase is 'My Beloved is Mine and I am His' from the Song of Songs (2:16). This phrase and the meaning behind it have sustained me through many dark and difficult times of my life; doubt, depression, bereavement and temptation to leave the monastery. It links with one of the antiphons which I sang at my Solemn Profession on Easter Thursday, 1976: 'I am married to him whom angels serve, sun and moon marvel at his beauty'.

As I recite the psalms in choir, listen to the readings at the Divine Office and at Mass and to homilies, I receive surprising insights into words I've heard hundreds of times. They come also in many other ways, through novels, conversations with people inside and outside the monastery, even through the media, especially through hearing stories of the lives of other people.

In preparation for our last abbatial election we had a long series of meetings with two facilitators which included much reflection on the Word of God. On one occasion, the passage given us included Jesus cursing the barren fig tree although it was not the season for figs (Lk 13:6-9). My reflection on this linked it with the fig tree in the Song of Songs 'forming its first figs' in the spring; and it came to me that in the monastic life it is always the season for love, always the season for fruitfulness (Sg 2:13).

Recently at Vigils I was struck by the line in the long historical Psalm 105: 'they broke their marriage bond with the Lord' (v. 39). Later, when I was praying silently, the words from the marriage vows came into my mind: 'with my body I thee worship', and I made a connexion with our custom of bowing deeply after each psalm, as St Benedict recommends 'in honour and reverence for the Holy Trinity' (RB 9:7). I am now trying to do this in a much more conscious way.

Each day I receive Bishop Barron's short reflection on the Gospel of the day. Today, May 26th, he reminded us that in the Paschal Mystery Jesus consummates His marriage with His people, individually and collectively, an intimate union renewed each day in the Eucharist, in our encounter with the Word through Lectio Divina and in our love of each other.

'LONG BEFORE I SAW THE LORD, HE SAW ME'

Fernanda Streeter Walker
Manquehue Apostolic Movement

My name is Fernanda Streeter Walker and I have seen the Lord. I am also a person who has found happiness and is truly grateful for her life, with all the moments and experiences, all the feelings, the falls and getting ups, the deserts and the oases, the laughs and cries, everything that my life is made of. I am truly grateful for everything.

The first thing that came to my mind when I considered where I have seen the Lord, is my family. I have one sister and two brothers and, with my parents, they are my favorite people. I know that God thought exactly of the family where I had to be born and made it a great gift. It is here where I have had my very first experience of community, of tutoria, of joy that could only come from God.

I grew up in a really happy environment, in a school where I felt loved and made precious friendships that I am thankful for every day. Colegio San Benito gave me my academic education, but most importantly, it opened my eyes to a caring, thoughtful, paternal and loving God. My school introduced Him to me as a friend, as someone that would be always there for me, that would never desert me. Because of Manquehue, I knew how I could find this perfect God: through Lectio. And I think that this fact – that He is alive (not just an old man that once was important in history), that He is reachable, that He speaks and that I can be with Him – changed my life forever, in ways that I can still not describe or even understand.

The thing is, that long before I saw the Lord, He saw me. He saw me with all my flaws, all my insecurities, all my doubts, and even then, He loved me. He saw me and even, before I knew myself, He knew me. I discovered this in Rio de Janeiro, at World Youth Day in 2013, when I felt God speaking directly to me through the words He spoke once to Jeremiah: 'Before I formed you in the womb I knew you; before you came to birth I consecrated you; I appointed you as prophet to the nations.' (Jr 1:5) Knowing that He sees me everyday and knows my sins, knows that every day I choose other things before Him, that I don't always feel like praying, that I forget Him – knowing all this, He sees me and still loves me and wants to speak to me. I just feel that I am His favorite.

In 2015, I began my studies to become a lawyer. Now I am about to finish it, but the first year was pretty difficult for me. I found myself humiliated and frustrated, and at the end of that year I realised that I missed God. I missed putting my trust in Him and not in myself – it is exhausting thinking that I am the only one that has to know the answers and have the strength for everything. I rest so much when I trust Him! This is a daily challenge, that my personality makes a little bit harder...

After two years of missing God, I decided to go to Portsmouth Abbey on a mission with Manquehue. It was there that I came to know for sure that God wasn't a phase of my life, or a hobby or something that after a while would pass. God is not replaceable. In Portsmouth I realised the meaning of my baptism: I am forever marked with an indelible seal. Even when I move away from Him, He will always be there for me. This changed my life again, as did the further knowledge that this seal isn't a scar that I want or need to hide: it is a shiny beautiful seal that everyone should see, in fact, that I have the mission to share.

This vocation to 'share my baptism' made me go to Downside School in England a while later. Looking back, I realise that it was really the Spirit who made this decision for me – it was not one I could have made at the time on my own strength; rather, I became an instrument of His mission. At Downside I learned about God's time: that it has nothing to do with my own timing, plans or ideals. It's just how Peter said: 'But there is one thing, my dear friends, that you must never forget: that with the Lord, a day is like a thousand years, and a thousand years are like a day.' (2 P 3:8) I couldn't ignore this: one second of silence with Him could change the story of my life forever and five months (that was my time in England) are like one second if I am with Him. Trusting in His time was really difficult for me, I doubted a lot before going because many people didn't understand me, even I didn't understand it so well, but I felt this fire inside me that made me ignore my humans doubts and follow Him. And He answered me, with miracles, with daily gifts, with angels, smiles, conversions, deep prayers and a loving community. He answered and gave me spiritual eyes to see that I have seen the Lord.

The gift of these experiences are wrapped in a mystery. The mystery of a God that, for our sake, became human and accepted suffering, and even death on a cross, so that we might find true life in Him. It is by faith in this mystery that a group of women decided to build a community to evangelise, both in Portsmouth and in Downside. I am grateful to have seen the power of a community built in this mystery. It is in these communities that I opened my eyes to the wonder of the human being, and the wonder of discovering who I am. With their echoes I understood my echoes, with their sufferings I understood my sufferings, with their joys I celebrated my own joys, in a way that is difficult to describe, in a mysterious way that made us share one big echo, one suffering, one joy; everything was one with us in Christ.

It is hard to summarise where or how I have seen the Lord because I strongly believe in a God of details, an artisan. These experiences taught me how to focus my eyes better and get close enough to see the masterpiece that is my life. I have seen the Lord in my friendships, in people that are chosen by Him to appear in my life. I have seen Him when I fall and He gives me the strength to get up again. I have seen Him in the quiet peace of silence. I have seen Him in the small details of things:

when I am studying – making me love my profession – and in a good conversation with a cup of coffee. In a smile in the face of sufferings. I have seen the Lord in my Lectio groups throughout the years and when the bus stops just in time. I strongly believe in a God of details.

I wrote this after being a while away from God, having difficulties to pray, in a desert of faith. But nothing of what I just wrote has changed: I have seen the Lord! I have seen Him in my family; I have seen Him loving and knowing me, showing me that His time is the perfect time; I have seen Him in beautiful communities; but most importantly, I have seen Him and felt Him in my own heart. That is a fact that would never change, even if I wanted to. He lives in me.

FINDING CHRIST'S COMMUNITY

Joseph Meehan
The Weave of Manquehue Prayer

'He said to them, "But who do you say that I am?"' (Mt 16:15). This verse struck me this week as we prepare to celebrate the feast of St Peter and St Paul. Jesus asks the disciples a direct question, not what other people thought or what public opinion was, but what they, as individuals, thought. During a time when we have been unable to go to church or receive the sacraments as usual, for me this verse was a reminder of that calling from God to have a close relationship with Him and to remember that He knows me personally as an individual. Similarly, it was an invitation for me to place my trust in God fully and to take ownership of my faith.

My name is Joseph and I am currently studying Civil Engineering at Bristol University. I am in my second year and I was first introduced to Lectio last year; since then it has become an integral part of my faith and life.

I originally come from near Birmingham. Growing up, my faith always seemed important to me, but unfortunately my parish was primarily composed of middle aged and older people; there were no people my age and although my parish is very friendly and welcoming, I often struggled to find the community that Jesus talks about in the Gospel represented for me. Likewise, the only real experience of the Gospel that I had until coming to University was hearing the Gospel every Sunday at mass. I went to state secondary, so I did not have faith in common with any of my friends growing up. These were all excuses in some ways. Ultimately, I was caught up with being self-centred, lacked the effort and wanting a comfortable life for myself; therefore, my relationship with God was reserved for one hour on a Sunday.

When I came to Bristol, I joined the Catholic Society and it was there that my faith was refreshed. Seeing young people practising their faith was so encouraging and inspiring to me, and really helped to strengthen my own faith. It made me feel that it was not something that I should be ashamed of or just keep to myself, but instead something that I should cherish, share and develop.

It was at the Bristol CathSoc that I started to go to Lectio Divina. After mass every Sunday evening, there would be announcements for the upcoming week, and Lectio would always be one of them. Although it interested me, I was nervous about going, so put it off until one day I decided to take the plunge and turn up on a Wednesday evening.

I had never heard of Lectio Divina before, let alone taken part in it, nor had I ever really experienced anything like it. What struck me the most about that first experience of Lectio was the deep and meaningful feeling of fellowship and community. Even though I did not know any of the members personally prior to joining, I instantly felt welcomed and part of a warm community. It was just during the Autumn term that I first went, and I would hear stories about previous members of the Lectio Group, and it felt as if I knew them as well. The people I met at Lectio were not like anybody I had met before. Instead they were people who you could tell lived and experienced Christ through the Gospel and I could tell this by the way they acted and behaved.

Once I started sharing my echoes, I began to understand the great value that Lectio Divina has for me. I could articulate the way that God speaks to me through the Gospel in a way that I had never been able to do before.

For me, Lectio is a place I can go and forget about the worries and stresses of student life, the coursework deadlines and social pressures. I am reminded of the verse, 'Therefore do not worry about tomorrow, for tomorrow will worry about itself. Each day has enough trouble of its own.' (Mt 6: 34) Instead, I can focus on my relationship with God as part of a community of faith, reflecting on what role the Gospel has in my life and how God speaks to me. Lectio allows me to contemplate the Gospel in a prayerful setting amongst friends, which is something that I had not been able to do before coming to university. I can identify how the Gospel teachings apply to my life and especially to being a student at university.

Earlier this year, my family experienced two bereavements; my grandad and grandma passed away in the space of four months. This was a difficult time for me, especially with the additional stresses of University exams and coursework. I remember feeling like everything was crashing down around me, and often it was very easy to lose hope and motivation. For me, it was very easy to fall into an apathetic viewpoint and fail to see the value of the world. I also had difficulties with flatmates and friend groups. It was during this time that I found Lectio to be especially powerful, and in many ways, it was a lifeline and sanctuary for me. 'May the God of hope fill you with all joy and peace as you trust in Him, so that you may overflow with hope by the power of the Holy Spirit.' (Rm 15:13) I remember going to Lectio every Wednesday and knowing that I could find reassurance in the Gospel and share my feelings and difficulties. Even though I was away from home, it felt as if I had a family at Bristol. Although I do not think I realised it at the time, Lectio was very powerful in helping me to get through this time, through the Word of God but also through the community surrounding Lectio.

Now, after just over a year of attending Lectio; lots of the old members of the group have moved on. Some have graduated, others have other commitments with work. I have taken the role of leading the Lectio group, something that is daunting, but also very valuable. My own experience at Lectio has changed my outlook on life. I strive to have that optimism and show the love that God shows to me. 'But love your enemies, do good to them, and lend to them without expecting to get anything back. Then your reward will be great, and you will be children of the Most High, because he is kind to the ungrateful and wicked.' (Lk 6:35) For me, this verse reminds me of the love that God shows for me, and that no matter how far I seem to stray from God, He is still kind to me and wants to bring me closer to Him.

Since March, the UK has been affected by Covid 19 and lockdown, which has made spiritual life for everyone different and perhaps also difficult. In my case, not being able to receive the sacraments at Mass and not having that immediate community was hard to get used to, and often it was easy to feel abandoned and alone. One verse which gave me encouragement recently was Matthew 10, verse 31, 'So do not be afraid; you are worth more than many sparrows.' I know that God cares and looks after me in the time of crisis, and I am reminded that He knows me as a person. By placing my trust fully in God, I can also know Him personally. Every week, members of our lectio group have been meeting via video call to catch up, talk, and pray together. Even though we are separated physically, I know and trust that God is there with us, 'For where two or three have gathered together in My name, I am there in their midst.' (Mt 18:20)

'I WILL RUN THE WAY OF YOUR COMMANDS' (Ps 119:32)

Fr Chad Boulton OSB
Ampleforth Abbey

It felt like an arrest, an arm on the shoulder, stopping me in my tracks. The preacher's text was familiar: 'anyone who loses his life for my sake will find it' (Mt 16:25). I was sixteen and my life had been focused on studies and sport at an intensely competitive school: suddenly it seemed as if I had been wearing blinkers. The preacher took the story of Naaman: 'find your Jordan and jump in'. It was both exciting and frightening, as though God were asking me to sign a blank cheque, without specifying what I would have to pay. All I could sense was that God might one day ask me to be a monk.

I'm still not clear where all this had come from. I had been brought up in an Anglican family. My family roots were Quaker and Huguenot rather than Catholic. Perhaps it was my A-level study of the medieval church, perhaps it was my parents baptising me Benedict. But thirty years on, the most convincing, and disturbing, explanation is to see this as the same call that once went out to fishermen and tax collectors: 'You did not choose me. No, I chose you' (Jn 15:16).

It would, however, take ten years for the blank cheque to be cashed and for me to enter Ampleforth Abbey: in the meantime I acquired a certain reputation for angst. In many ways my family, my education and my health had provided a very privileged start in life and the classic recipe for middle-class guilt. Growing up in 1970s London, however, had not been an upbeat experience: the glass seemed half-empty, a society with decreasing joy, hope and trust. At best, like Benedict, I felt the need to return to the source, to find the springs that could renew. At worst, like Jonah, I felt the impulse to run away and hide. But even here, like Jonah, I discovered the relentlessness of God's mercy. Paul was right to glory in his weaknesses: they do become the avenues of grace.

I ran away from religion, headed off to the far end of the country and got a job in hospital administration in Carlisle. This was a time of blind, sometimes desperate, prayer: 'Your will be done', repeated amidst the diversions and distractions of life for a twenty-something, intensified when I moved to London. My prayers seemed like dots placed on a page, seemingly random at the time, only in retrospect revealing the shape and curve of a vocation. Finally, in 1991, I made a first decision and headed up to Ampleforth. Creeping to the cross on Good Friday roused the ancestral voices within to one final challenge but, after twenty four hours of turbulence, I was received into the Catholic Church at the Easter vigil. I never felt that I was required to deny my Anglican upbringing, to which I owed the foundations of my faith. A vocation is never from scratch and I always felt that I was bringing my Anglican inheritance with me.

A second decision now confronted me. On a grey Saturday in January the following year, saying evening prayer in my South London bedsit, I saw clearly that I had one life to lead and that seeking God mattered more than the career and marriage I was still looking to establish. Three months later, after talking things through with my parents, I gave in my notice at work.

In joining the Ampleforth community, which was busily pastoral rather than strictly contemplative, I was attracted by the combination of a monastic and a priestly vocation – becoming first a monk, a 'brother', and then a priest, a 'father', as a secondary step. During my novitiate I was discerning my vocation to both of these roles. I can remember in that time, during the feast of the Sacred Heart, praying, 'of course you can have my heart, but why here?' and then hearing, 'do you think it is a coincidence that you can give your heart here?'

After a year as a novice, I took temporary vows for three years, at the end of which I was free either to take permanent vows, or to leave. I nearly left, feeling that the 'magic' had gone and making plans for a new future. Standing at the door of the monastery, however, I found that there still remained outside me a call to stay, even though there was no desire within. It was a strange way to discover that my vocation was not dependent on my feelings: 'not my will but yours be done' (Lk 22:42).

Two years later I was ordained a priest. The Ordination itself was a day of extraordinary happiness – my younger brother was even moved to propose to his girlfriend immediately afterwards. Six of us were priested by Cardinal Hume, in the year before he died. At the point where the priests laid their hands on me, all I could see with my head bowed was a succession of anonymous shoes going past, as though the gift being passed on was independent of any particular personality. I can still remember the overwhelming sense of affirmation when first the Cardinal and then a succession of family, friends and brethren all knelt down asking for my blessing.

The reality since then, of course, has not maintained that level of intensity. Once the various steps of monastic profession and priestly ordination are over, there is the almost unavoidable sense of a plateau. Priesthood in a monastery is often a latent gift, exercised when opportunities arise. Monasticism can become the private faith of cohabiting spiritual bachelors. But God invites us as we are, to give what we can: St Paul VI called for witnesses, not teachers, and the vocation of a monk-priest is to be a faithful witness to the gospel by living out the Benedictine rule. Learning how to love is perhaps the greatest challenge.

The strong moments are when the water flows and the fire burns, when as a priest you are invited into people's lives and when as a priest you are available to honour that trust. There have been more than enough regrets, infidelities, negligences, shortcuts. But stronger still is a recurring sense of God's mercy, and a surprisingly unshakeable sense of God's choice.

Before my first homily, an older priest advised me to ask: 'am I preaching myself or am I preaching Christ?' The mystery of this vocation is that ultimately it is not about my performance and not in my control. St John XXIII would remind himself each night: 'remember, Angelo, you're not running this show.'

What helped me to join the monastery was this counsel from Rahner: 'there is no human freedom without decision – a man who wants everything never makes a choice and never really gets hold of anything.' I wonder today whether we are so concerned to keep our options open that we never exercise them. We are afraid of failing so we avoid commitment. That was certainly why it took me so long to make a final decision. What matters is what we are free for, rather than what we are free from, something the psalmist understood. 'I will run the way of your commands; you give freedom to my heart.' (Ps 119:32)

'PEACE BE WITH YOU' (Jn 20:19)

Paola Felipes
The Weave of Manquehue Prayer

N.B. I am submitting this testimony in 2020, around three years after writing it. I thought about writing a new one of a more recent experience, but I did not want to discard the experience detailed in this testimony. Reading this now and looking back, I can definitely pinpoint this time as the point at which my faith took a real leap and I know Lectio had a lot to do with that as it allowed me to get closer to God and develop my relationship with Him. Despite not being recent, this testimony describes what was a real and important experience for me, therefore I believe it still has value and can resonate with others.

I have just finished my first year studying at the University of Bath, a new experience coming with tough personal challenges. Nevertheless, through it, I have clung to my faith. I realise that at every stage in life there will be difficulties, but it is all part of my journey and in fact it is during hard times that I have felt God's presence most strongly. He gives me the strength to cope. I have been doing Lectio sometimes with my university Catholic Society but not often. Recently I have been struggling to pray and wondering what I could do about it. Then I get asked out of the blue about submitting this old testimony and, upon reading it back, I realise what an important part of my prayer life Lectio was, so I now want to try and make the effort to do it regularly because I know how good it is for my faith and that when I do it I love it. The Lord works in mysterious ways!

MY TESTIMONY

I am Paola Felipes, I am seventeen years old and a student at Ampleforth College. I am currently studying Economics, Spanish and Business Studies at A Level. I am looking to take a gap year travelling through South America and working at home in Gibraltar before studying a business degree with Spanish. I come from a Catholic family of seven and have grown up in Gibraltar. I came to Ampleforth in September 2016 where I joined a Lectio Divina group and met the members of St Columba, the Manquehue community resident here. I then became a Lectio Leader for the Year 10s in my School House. I really enjoy Lectio Divina and love the Emmaus community which I belong to. At the moment I am finding it difficult to transmit this through to the members of the group I am leading. This troubles me sometimes, as I want to give them the same experience that I receive in my own group.

Nevertheless, I hope that with time and more experience we can become a closer group, both in listening and discussing the gospel, and also in friendship.

What I have most appreciated from moving to this school is finding, in my Lectio groups and through other activities in school, people with the same faith as me. This has helped to strengthen my relationship with God, knowing that there are people with the same beliefs, going through similar or different struggles with their faith. Through listening I have seen God's light in other people and the presence of Jesus in everyone has become much clearer. I am especially moved when young members of my own Lectio group share their feelings on the Gospel readings with everyone, as it is safe to say that children of that age find it harder to express themselves in such a way, as they are perhaps concerned about what people may think of them. My Lectio groups have also encouraged me to pray to the Holy Spirit, which had never really been part of my thoughts or prayers before because I never fully understood it. However, it is now that I realise the significance of the gift of the Holy Spirit, the living God, in guiding me through my everyday life and opening my heart to other people and to the Gospel readings.

Since moving to this school, there is no doubt that I have experienced some difficult times. Moving to a new country, leaving my family, whom I am very close to, behind, adapting to a new school and making new friends. At first, I thought it was the wrong decision as I began encountering these problems, which I had not anticipated. This made me lose faith at first as I prayed to God for help, but my problems seemed to continue, and I became a weaker person. I let the busy school life here overwhelm me too much and the only thing I could think of was finding a way to escape these problems (one of my many faults is that I over-worry). However, I spoke to my father at home whom I respect very much, and he gave me words of understanding, comfort and advice. At the time, our family had also been experiencing sad and challenging times for two years and is still facing difficulties. Upon my return to school later on, with my father's advice in mind, I approached things in a different light. I joined a Lectio Divina group and here I felt part of a welcoming community and made more friends. It gave me the chance also to reflect on my faith and allow Jesus into my life again.

Different people may find God in different ways, and for me Lectio, although important, has just been one part of this continuing journey of finding myself and finding God. Instead of asking for my problems to disappear, I thanked God for my blessings, I prayed for my family, my friends, and asked God for guidance in my life; but most of all, I learnt to place my trust in Him. When I have days where I feel it is all too much, these are the times when I know that I will be able to get everything done with God by my side. This is when I stop worrying, have faith, pray to God for strength and start again, placing my trust in Him and receiving a renewed Grace.

Of course, throughout our lives it is not always going to be an easy ride. We will have to make tough decisions and go through difficult experiences; however, we must realise that having faith will not make these problems disappear, but what it will do is make the load lighter. When we feel like something is really worrying us, leave it in the hands of God and receive comfort and peace from this. When we really want something, but we don't get it, trust that God is showing us that in the end it will be for the better. When we have to make a decision, talk to God and listen to His word, and ask for guidance to make the right decision. And when we are going through difficult times, remember all the things we have to be thankful for, pray to the Holy Spirit for strength and try to see the good, simple things in people and in life because times will get better and life is too short to over-worry. Make time for people, respect them, listen and try to see Jesus in them, as this will give you hope and light – I have found this hard but very powerful and encouraging at times. Surround yourself with the people you love and who give you joy, but also be kind to those who are alone and in need or those you do not get along well with and remember Jesus' prime commandments; 'love each other as I have loved you', and 'love God above all else' (Mt 22:36-40).

Most importantly, the encouragement and comfort I have received is in realising that Christ is alive and loves me and wants to be part of my life, if I open my heart to Him and allow Him to be in it too. In the future I look to continue strengthening my relationship with God and growing closer to Him in faith. I hope to continue with Lectio groups later in life and remain in contact with those who have given me this gift and with the friends I have made through it.

'SURELY THE LORD IS IN THIS PLACE, AND I WAS NOT AWARE OF IT'
(Gn 28:16)

Martín Rosselot Saavedra
Manquehue Apostolic Movement

My name is Martin Rosselot, I am nineteen years old, a former student of San Benito (one of the three schools of the Manquehue Apostolic Movement) and I am studying Civil Engineering. I am currently living with the St. Scholastica community in Downside, England. I came to receive formation in the community and be part of the mission of St. Scholastica in this school. However, the mysterious action of God brought me at this time when the Coronavirus has prevented the schools from functioning normally, so my stay has been very different to what I expected. It has brought me to recognise how Christ has been teaching me humility throughout my whole life, to help me to recognise my need for Him, and seek Him out. To explain how, I must first go back to when I was still a student at my school.

In general, I have had a very peaceful and happy life. I have a family that I love very much and with whom I feel very comfortable. However, at the age of thirteen I reached a sort of 'crisis' point in my life. Throughout my childhood, I always had a mentality of following in the footsteps of others. I thought that life was about being as normal as possible, thinking like most people, doing what everyone else does. I felt that if I didn't do what everyone else was doing, I was failing.

Aged thirteen, what was 'normal' stopped being so obvious to me. It was a time when everyone was starting to become more independent, and in this independence I felt a greater pressure to discern, for myself, exactly what I was meant to be doing, what I 'had' to do. I felt a little lost. Deep down I was asking myself why I existed, what my purpose was. The only thing I knew was that I had to study and try to get good grades, but, I questioned, in the time I wasn't studying, what did I have to do?

I don't remember how, but little by little I concluded: 'I'm not going to bother anyone'. I felt I could only do something if it didn't negatively affect or displease anyone. For me, that became my only purpose. It was not such an awful purpose, and I didn't have a bad time; life just looked a little 'ugly'.

At this time the older students began to have a great impact on me. I saw something in them that I wanted too. They told how they went against the current, how they had found something that made them very happy, how they didn't care about the looks of others, how they had something to aim for in their life. All this led me to seek to get closer to God in my Lectio group, in the missions and in tutoría.

A very important moment for me was a retreat in Fourth Form. The theme was Encountering Christ. The testimonies shared with me by older students, alumni and teachers touched me deeply. They told me how they could give their lives for Christ after having encounters with Him similar to those recounted in this book. Their testimony was proof to me that Christ existed.

I began to find happiness, especially in service. My purpose enlarged from simply seeking not to disturb others, to actively trying to be of service. And this not only left me calm, but made me happy. In serving others, I too found Christ, in love, in making myself a servant. I felt fulfilled, I knew what I had to do, what I had to aim for.

And now we come to the significance of the present. I came here to England to work in the school, to live in the community and to travel a little. I arrived here and the reality was completely different. But if it hadn't been for the temporary closure of the schools and the fact that we couldn't go and travel around England, we wouldn't have had so much time for community life and formation. It wouldn't have been my turn to prepare a formation session for the community, on humility.

To prepare the formation I studied Manquehue documents that expound Chapter Seven of St Benedict's Rule on 'The value of humility'. There were some things that caught my attention and really let God speak to me. For example, that Christ's way of saving us 'is a path of self-emptying, persecution, suffering and humiliation, a humiliation that culminates with death on a cross' (WUG 331) or that 'God allows cracks to appear in our lives and shatters our certainties so that we return to him.' (WUG 328) Finally, St Benedict talks a lot about 'Jacob's ladder', a ladder dreamt of by Jacob in the old Testament, upon which 'angels of God were shown to him going up and down in a constant exchange between heaven and earth' (RB 7:6). In this dream God promises Jacob that He is with him and will never abandon him (Gn 28:15). St Benedict sees Jacob's ladder as a ladder of humility, in which every downward step of humility that the soul makes is really an upward step towards God. I discovered that this ladder, this encounter with the presence of God, is 'in the interior of each one of us, what we call the inner cloister, it is where we become aware of the presence of the Holy Spirit dwelling in us.' (WUG 339)

If I hadn't prepared the session on humility, I would not have understood that humility is the path that Jesus teaches. I would not have understood that being Christian is to be humble of heart, that is, giving up everything to let God consume me. And most importantly, I would have not understood that all the experiences I have described above were indeed the work of Christ, humbling me to attract me to Himself.

Yes, before, I was aware that Christ had acted, but I never knew that it was He who had taken away all my 'certainties' so that when I was there, not knowing what to do, I would go to Him. I used to see things with the perspective that every time I went away from God I had a bad time, and if I came closer, I was happy. But no, Christ humbled me, made me 'have a hard time' to draw me to Him. At every moment I was in His action, in His perfect plan. The 'ugly' moments were also part of His action. He made his way of salvation with me as with the people of Israel: 'He humbled you, causing you to hunger and then feeding you with manna, which neither you nor your ancestors had known, to teach you that man does not live on bread alone but on every word that comes from the mouth of the Lord.' (Dt 8:3) It was Christ who in my fourth form retreat, through my tutors, my teachers and my close friends, told me: "I am the Way; I am Truth and Life" (Jn 14:6).

The happiness that listening to God brought me, of understanding His way of salvation with me, was enormous. It was like the satisfaction that solving a problem brings you; reaching an answer, but better, since the answer is not to some temporary problem, it is the solution of my life, all I need to know: Christ loves me in my smallness, especially in my smallness, so I have to make myself small or recognise my smallness, in order to recognise the greatness of God in me.

In the experiences of my life, Christ has given me the impulse to follow his path of humility, and in recognising this, I am invited each day to take it up. He also invites me to look at every moment and place as Jacob looks at the cave and the stone on which he slept when God shows him the ladder, which for St. Benedict is a ladder of humility: 'When Jacob awoke from his sleep, he thought, "Surely the Lord is in this place, and I was not aware of it". He was afraid and said, "How awesome is this place! This is none other than the house of God; this is the gate of heaven."' (Gn 28:16-17).

'IN A MOMENT OF QUIET AND WITHOUT DRAMA'

Fr Francis Dobson OSB
Ampleforth Abbey

1960 was a difficult year, and my father John Ignatius was dying and did die on the Feast of St Ignatius of Antioch on the 17th of October. But earlier that year, in February, I went with my father and mother for my first visit to Westminster Cathedral. We did not live in London, and in those post-war years of austerity made only a few visits there. But that day, I came to the Cathedral. My father had been meeting his physician, also my godfather, who lived next to the Cathedral. It was a weekday, the Cathedral was quiet, and I think we walked around the chapels, and to the Chapel of Our Lady, and then to the other side, to the chapel of the Blessed Sacrament. In crossing from the Chapel of Our Lady to the Blessed Sacrament, there were ropes that had to be lifted to pass, and someone held the rope for us to pass – and somehow it was important and I saw the Lord.

It was not in any individual or word, but somehow in the situation, in lots of things together. There was this moment of service, of the one holding the rope, but it was not that. There was the quiet and sense of prayer, the hush and faith, but it was not that. There was the air or atmosphere of something of the mystery of faith, the beauty of the pillars and brick, ceilings, chapels, mosaics and murals, the fantastic sense of the Byzantine and the dark, but it was not that. Perhaps, yes, it was all that, I don't know, and it was something beyond. It was finding the faith of my young years, and I think, I wonder, I saw the Lord. I loved Jesus, I prayed to Our Lady, I went to Mass, and now in a moment of quiet and without drama, I saw the Lord.

Over the years, there are many moments and experiences which have been moments I was anointed by the sense that I saw the Lord. There was the prayer of each day. There was the beauty of other times and people and Cathedrals – not just bricks and air, but meeting the Lord in life – such as the Basilica of St Pius X in Lourdes, here finding the presence of Jesus, and my own Abbey Church at Ampleforth, where I came first on the 9th of September 1961, the day after it was opened. But this moment at Westminster Cathedral was a meeting with the Lord; in a few seconds, I was blessed and brought to love and to new faith and hope in the presence of Jesus – and I saw the Lord.

Over the years that followed that encounter there, Westminster Cathedral came to play a beautiful and strong role in my Catholic everyday life. In my twenties, it was my parish. Later, at the Cathedral, I worked and prayed with a group of young persons with the Legion of Mary, about ten or fifteen of us, serving the very poor parish and its people, whom we learnt to love.

The Cathedral was this home to those who pray, for the baptised, those who gently accept faith. There was the early morning Mass, and often a sacristan came to take you away to serve at one of the side chapels, perhaps the Chapel of St George and the English Martyrs, with the body of St John Southworth, the English martyr of 1654 – I would visit his tomb each day. Sometimes one went to the Crypt to serve Mass, with the Hats of former Cardinals hanging. There was the Shrine of Our Lady of Westminster, the Stations of the Cross of Eric Gill, the liturgies of the great feasts, the Cathedral Choir, Holy Week. I came to love the building itself, the Cathedral of the Precious Blood – its Byzantine history, marble, mosaics, walls, darkness , its stone and brick – perhaps on that first visit I sensed it, but did not yet understand.

That first day in Westminster Cathedral was one when Jesus welcomed me, anointed me, greeted me, and I stood with Mary at the Foot of the Cross. Jesus spoke and said to me 'This is your Mother' (Jn 19:26). Surely also, it was an experience of being like Mary at the Annunciation, who says 'Let what you have said be done to me' (Lk 1:38). And it was as at Emmaus, to have been walking as the two disciples with a stranger, and, suddenly, have one's eyes opened to recognise Jesus in 'the breaking of bread' (Lk 24:30-31). Along the road, I did not know who walked with me, and now in this moment in Westminster Cathedral, my eyes were opened and I recognised Jesus, I saw the Lord. The Monastic Vows were themselves a special moment when I saw the Lord, as I lay on the black Pall on the Feast of the Triumph of the Holy Cross in 1968, but in February 1960, in Westminster Cathedral, Jesus spoke to me and I saw the Lord.

N.B. Fr Francis Dobson passed away on the 9th of January, 2018, in the 79th year of his age, the 51st of his monastic life, and the 42nd of his priesthood. A friend of the Manquehue community and of the Weave, he wrote this testimony upon their request in 2017.

GLOSSARY

Conversatio Morum
Latin for 'conversion of manners', meaning broadly 'to change in order to behave as a monk should'. It is one of the three commitments, together with stability and obedience, that St Benedict asks a monk to take when making his monastic profession.

Divine Office
Liturgy marking the hours of each day and sanctifying it. It usually includes seven 'hours' consisting mainly in the singing of psalms and other texts from Scripture. Celebrated in choir, it is a main feature of Benedictine life. It is also known as 'Liturgy of the Hours.'

Echo
What someone says to share with others how God has spoken personally to them through a passage from Scripture.

It is the resonance of Scripture in someone's life. Echoes are done in the first person singular and they are listened to in silence by the rest of the group.

Escuela de Servicio
Spanish for 'School of Service' (cf RB P: 45) In Manquehue Schools it refers to a community of students and alumni who work together to raise awareness about social issues and lead the school community to reach out to people in need.

Forerunner (Worth)
The Forerunners are a team of youth ministers who work in collaboration with the monastic community and chaplains at Worth School in Sussex.

Lectio Divina
Latin for 'reading God'. It is a way of prayerfully reading the Bible and engaging through it in a personal relationship with the Lord. Its roots are in the Old and New Testaments and in the Fathers of the Church. A daily monastic practice, it is also recommended for all Christians.

Manquehue
A mountain in Santiago de Chile. Pronounced Man-keh-weh, it means 'place of the condor' in the native language. In the book, Manquehue is usually used as short for Manquehue Apostolic Movement.

Manquehue Apostolic Movement

A lay Benedictine community originated in Santiago de Chile. Its life breath is Lectio Divina and the cultivation of spiritual friendship. Manquehue has a long standing relationship with English Benedictine monasteries and schools.

The Weave of Manquehue Prayer

A network of friends that seek to help one another to pray, cultivate spiritual friendship, and share with many the Good News of the Risen Christ. Based in the UK, the Weave draws from the Manquehue charism to enrich initiatives of evangelisation and service.

Colegios (San Benito, San Lorenzo, San Anselmo)

Spanish for 'schools.' In the book it normally refers to the three Manquehue schools in Santiago de Chile: San Benito, San Lorenzo and San Anselmo. These schools are Manquehue's main work and their aim is the evangelisation of students, teachers, staff and families.

Oblate

A member of Manquehue with a life commitment to the community. There are cenobite and married oblates, both male and female. They are all lay members of the Church, not priests or religious.

San José/ Patagonia

Manquehue's Formation Centre in Chilean Patagonia. Located in a stunning and remote part of the country, it offers young adults a four months experience of community life and formation. It also welcomes others, school students and adults, for shorter retreats.

Manquehue Scouts

A particular way of the scout path marked by the Manquehue charism. Manquehue Scout Groups are associated with Manquehue Schools and include students, alumni, boys and girls. They are a privileged space for 'tutoría'.

Trabajos y Misiones

Spanish for 'Works and Missions.' A week or ten days during summer or winter holidays, when students led by alumni go out to rural areas to live, pray and work together. They build simple houses for people in need and visit people to share the Gospel with them.

Tutoría

Spanish for 'mentoring.' In Manquehue, it refers to the friendship between older students or alumni and younger ones, seeking to share with them their experience of God, prayer and service. Tutoría is warmly welcoming others in Christ and it also happens in other age groups.

World Youth Day (WYD)

A worldwide encounter with the Pope celebrated about every three years in a different country. WYDs were started by Pope St John Paul II and they gather millions of young people in a festive atmosphere centred in Jesus Christ.

ABBREVIATIONS

RB: Saint Benedict's Rule
Vs: verses
WUG: *Waking up to God* by José Manuel Eguiguren

BIBLE ABBREVIATIONS

Old Testament

New Testament

Gn: Genesis
Dt: Deuteronomy
2 Ch: 2 Chronicles
Ps: Psalms
Sg: Song of Songs
Is: Isaiah
Jr: Jeremiah
Ezk: Ezekiel
Zp: Zephaniah
Zc: Zechariah

Mt: Matthew
Mk: Mark
Lk: Luke
Jn: John
Ac: Acts
Rm: Romans
1 Co: 1 Corinthians
Ga: Galatians
Ep: Ephesians
Ph: Philippians
Col: Colossians
2 Tm: 2 Timothy
1 P: 1 Peter
1 Jn: 1 John

Printed in Great Britain
by Amazon